A C The OLLEGE PPLICATION E SSAY

The COLLEGE APPLICATION ESSAY

SARAH
MYERS
McGINTY

College Entrance Examination Board
New York

The College Board: Expanding College Opportunity

The College Board is a national nonprofit membership association dedicated to preparing, inspiring, and connecting students to college and opportunity. Founded in 1900, the association is composed of more than 3,900 schools, colleges, universities, and other educational organizations. Each year, the College Board serves over three million students and their parents, 22,000 high schools, and 3,500 colleges through major programs and services in college admission, guidance, assessment, financial aid, enrollment, and teaching and learning. Among its best-known programs are the SAT®, the PSAT/NMSQT™, the Advanced Placement Program® (AP®), and Pacesetter®. The College Board is committed to the principles of equity and excellence, and that commitment is embodied in all of its programs, services, activities, and concerns.

For further information, contact www.collegeboard.com.

In all of its book publishing activities the College Board endeavors to present the works of authors who are well qualified to write with authority on the subject at hand and to present accurate and timely information. However, the opinions, interpretations, and conclusions of the authors are their own and do not necessarily represent those of the College Board; nothing contained herein should be assumed to represent an official position of the College Board or any of its members.

Copies of this book are available from your local bookseller or may be ordered from College Board Publications, Box 886, New York, New York 10101. The price is $12.95, plus $4 for postage and handling. Purchase orders above $25 are accepted.

Editorial inquiries concerning this book should be directed to Guidance Publishing, The College Board, 45 Columbus Avenue, New York, New York 10023-6992.

Interior design by Marnie Ingman/Publications Services, The College Board.

Library of Congress Catalog Number: 97-068121
ISBN: 0-87447-575-9

Printed in the United States of America

For Pete's sake

Contents

Acknowledgments

For anyone who has studied and taught English, writing a book is a wonderfully humbling experience. There is, of course, what Matthew Arnold called "the best that is known and thought in the world," the entire history of British and American literature, with which to compare one's effort. And then there are all the teachers, colleagues, officemates, and mentors (including my eleventh-grade English teacher, a history teacher whose classes are said to embody the charm and wit of a good cocktail party, and a marathon vice-principal) who have preceded me, shared with me, and inspired me. And last there are the best teachers in the world, 20 years of high school students. Writing this book meant continual collision with something learned from someone else. I acknowledge and thank all these sources, especially my students, and most particularly those Millburn High School students in the class of 1975 and in the class of 1986. Of all who have passed through room 210, it was the one in the front of the class who learned the most and had the most fun!

I also want to thank those who have guided this book to publication, Carolyn Trager, first and foremost, and Maryann Brinley, Barbara Weller, and Sandra MacGowan—for their positive encouragement. Thanks also go to Nancy Donehower, Bill Hiss, Kristin Crowley, and all those involved in college admission—staffers and applicants—who shared with me their writing, their experiences, their insights. Thanks also to Bates College, Reed College, Ronald Etergino, Ellen Grosman, David Levi, Lindsay Grimm, Jonathan Levitt, Jon Schwanbeck, and Mark Millman for their contributions to Chapter 6.

Finally, I must acknowledge and thank John, J.W., Sarah, Bill, Phyllis, Dorothy, and Valari . . . they know why.

S. M. M.

1 Applying to College

My grandmother was a woman of vision and will. As the eldest child of nine she had to be—and she was *not* going to spend her whole life in Buffalo. Wherever her grit and determination came from, it inspired her, in 1905, to apply to Radcliffe, the women's college at Harvard. She wrote, "I'd like to come." They wrote back, "Come on Monday."

Many things were harder for women in those days, but it seems a few things were easier. In today's world, such a story seems remote, fantastic, and ideal. The college application process is now, like so much else, more complex. Students begin shaping their lives toward college at the beginning of adolescence. Parents have had it in mind from the first day of nursery school.

The process is also noticeably businesslike. It costs a few hundred dollars to travel around and see the colleges you might be interested in, to tour the campuses and have interviews. Add a few hundred dollars more for study books, a review course, tests, and applications. Some seniors will spend a few hundred dollars *more* to get private counseling, specialized advice, coaching for the interviews, help with the applications, or guidance with the essay. All of this is a preamble to the $10,000 to $30,000 a year college itself will cost.

Various companies market assistance. There are SAT review courses in many towns. Bookstores stock review and preparation guides. Publishers issue books on how to beat the tests, how to get into the right school, books full of Madison Avenue ideas like "packaging," "positioning," and "marketing" yourself—as if you were a commercial product jockeying for shelf position, flaunting an appetizing image.

The colleges, too, are eager to present an appealing picture. Many of them create glossy viewbooks, attractive college fair displays, and high school recruiting campaigns to attract top applicants to their campuses.

Many of the people involved in this process, however, lament these changes. Dr. Marlyn McGrath Lewis, director of admissions at Harvard University, describes the admission staff as a group of hard-working people "determined to bring to Harvard and Radcliffe students who are diverse in their talents and interests." But the more common perception is the one described by William C. Hiss, vice-president for administrative services at Bates College: "We are seen, wrongly I think, as a set of intellectual gatekeepers, moral judges, and protectors of the righteous who are already inside. Like Dante's *Divine Comedy,* we offer three possibilities: paradise, purgatory, and hell—that is, admit, wait-list, deny."

The anxiety that such a vision creates for high school students can be intense. To some, colleges seem to be the enemy; they scrutinize and choose without explanation. Acceptance patterns may seem capricious because colleges seek a *diverse* freshman class. There isn't always a clear distinction between The Elect and The Damned. Students who apply for early decision often become the focus of curiosity and concern for other seniors. "How did Jessica get in if Matt didn't?" Juniors carefully watch and analyze the springtime selection of those who precede them. "How could Harvard take Mark when Bowdoin didn't take Shareen?" And some, in moments of panic, conclude that no college is going to admit them. "Remember John last year? He didn't get in anywhere. Guidance was making pitiful phone calls for him all the way into June!"

Making Choices

The purpose of this book is to calm things down a little, because calming down and getting a bit of perspective eases the application process. Understanding the process reduces the anxiety. Knowledge is power. If you know what you're in for, if you know what you are supposed to do and how to do it, you can face the tasks with confidence.

First of all, the goal of this process is not to sell an ideal image of yourself. It is to find the right school for you. The process of choice is almost entirely yours. This is important. *You* are doing nearly all the decision making. Remember, colleges are themselves competing for students. You have much more control in this situation than you imagine. You've been gathering knowledge about colleges for a long time. You've heard of Harvard and Yale and Stanford . . . and the schools where Mom and Dad or your elder brother or the kid down the block went. You've begun a list of *your choices*. Your guidance counselor may help you add others, but it's your list.

You write for application packets and perhaps take a trip to see some of *your choices*. You narrow down the list, settle on the colleges that really suit you, and then apply to *your choices*—those you're convinced you could be happy at, including a "safety" and one or two "long shots." You are still doing all the choosing.

Then the applications are filed. It is only at this point that the choice is out of your hands. But assuming your selection of colleges is reasonable, you will probably be accepted at more than one school and, once again, the choice will be yours. Each one of the colleges is hopeful that *you* will accept *them!*

Keeping in mind that you're in charge should calm things down somewhat. Your goal is not to gain admission to the most academically grueling institution in America; it is to find a school where you can grow, learn, and succeed, a school where your special talents and interests will be appreciated and cultivated. You will make your choices with information from a wide range of sources:

- guidebooks
- catalogs, home pages, and literature from the colleges
- ExPAN or similar software
- reputation, word of mouth, media coverage
- alumni and other applicants from your high school
- guidance personnel, teachers, and other professionals
- college representatives at your high school
- campus visits and interviews

Working hard on your part of this job—researching the schools and preparing the applications—will make the part you don't control less threatening and unpredictable.

A close look at what you're not in charge of—the admission process—may help, too. Colleges are not looking for one type of student. As Dr. Lewis said, they are trying to put together a diverse community. Their goal is remarkably similar to yours: to find a successful match of school and student. It is interesting to compare the way you choose with the way the college chooses. The college relies on a much more focused set of resources:

- grades, class rank, and grade-point average
- course of study

- test scores
- biographical data (summer activities, jobs, special interests)
- recommendations
- an interview
- one or more essays
- where appropriate, supporting material (audition, portfolio)

Each of these elements contributes to the picture of you the college will examine and judge. Of course, the evaluation process differs at every school. Large universities and state schools may not enjoy the luxury of a personalized evaluation of each application. Some tax-supported state universities admit any state resident with passing grades and a high school diploma—Idaho, for example. California state schools declare minimums (for grades, grade-point average, rank in class, and so on) for admission. Other schools shun the numerical approach. The University of Michigan reviews 25,000 applications individually. Ted Spencer, director of admissions at Michigan, says, "Our admissions process is not like that of a small liberal arts college but we do not evaluate our applications with a computer; some applications are, in fact, evaluated three or four times." Colleges may rate applicants' personal and academic qualities, assigning numbers to each of these factors. Bennington, however, does not reduce any part of its applications to a number. All schools, even the large state universities that rely heavily on computers, have a special process for "gray zone" applications which may require additional readers or consideration by a committee. Every college makes its decisions in its own way.

The people who make these decisions also vary. The readers of applications are usually a combination of experienced senior admission personnel and younger staffers, often themselves recent graduates of the school. But faculty members may be part of the process. At Cal Tech, all admission decisions involve faculty. Oberlin, Reed, and Sarah Lawrence include student readers on admission committees. Applicants may also be looked at by specialists: music faculty hear auditions; art staff view portfolios. A dean of admission oversees everything.

The committee is not a nameless, faceless group of people, uniform in taste and attitude. It is made up of individuals. Assigned a seemingly endless pile of folders in the dark days of early spring, such an audience—overworked and tired—may find that a creative, innovative, interesting, or unique element in an application makes the difference. High scores and great grades do stand out. But students mistake their audience when they visualize a stuffy bunch of academics in search of an academic superstar. Peter Van Buskirk, director of admissions at Franklin and Marshall College, says, "We're not looking for one kind of student. A liberal arts college would be ill-advised to do that." There is no perfect applicant. Many things are sought within a class and many different elements make up the admission committee's final judgment. The folder is a web of information, a jigsaw puzzle that is interconnected and interactive. Each element plays its own part, each makes its own argument.

Your High School Record

The numbers come first. Colleges request grades beginning with ninth grade. Three and a half years of performance gives them a knowledge of your academic achievement and also a look at the pattern of your growth and progress. Straight A's are nice—but very rare in a challenging course of study. An improvement in grades is positive, too—the opposite will certainly raise eyebrows in the admission office. But above all other factors in the grade pattern, most colleges scrutinize the course load. A grade of B in Advanced Placement English is more important than an A in Chorus. An A in chemistry carries more weight than an A in civics. Dr. Erland D. Peterson, dean of admissions and records at Brigham Young University, describes how BYU considers course choices: "We add a factor to a student's grades for a strong educational program and for more challenging courses; we will consider up to 70 percent of the applicant's program in this way." Grades, class rank, and grade-point average are viewed in light of your course choices.

Grades, class rank, and grade-point average are also viewed in terms of your high school and its student body. Colleges assign regional responsibility to members of the admission staff who familiarize themselves with a few states or with one part of the country. They get to know the high schools and their course offerings. Some secondary schools have a reputation for excellence; others have less rigorous programs. Each school's general quality is considered in evaluating class rank and course of study.

Scores

A testing service also contributes numbers to your application. Schools usually require either the SAT I: Reasoning Test and SAT II: Subject Tests or the American College Testing Program Assessment (ACT). These standardized tests help admisssion personnel evaluate applicants' abilities relative to successful performance in college. The scores are seen as a yardstick with which students of widely differing backgrounds can be compared.

You probably took the PSAT/NMSQT or practiced with books like *10 Real SATs*. Some high schools offer SAT review courses as part of the curriculum and some students take a private review course. Familiarizing yourself with the various types of test questions can put you at ease and may make you a more efficient test taker.

The admission committee will look at your scores and compare them to your grades. High grades can overcome low scores but admission personnel will carefully scrutinize the course load and the high school's reputation. High scores can sometimes compensate for low grades, but that particular combination tends to make admission personnel nervous: Does the student lack motivation? Is she just a bright goof-off?

Grades, course load, grade-point average, class rank, and scores are the numerical information colleges use to evaluate an application. They look to your past as a clue to your future. Studies show that neither grades nor test scores alone indicate whether an applicant will succeed in college. However, the combination of high school record *and* scores has been found to be a fairly valid indicator of college success. College work also relies on the same study habits, self-discipline, skills, and personal qualities—enthusiasm, organization, independence of thought, responsibility, perseverance—that you need in high school. A lot of these qualities also contribute to success in a career.

Select colleges with all your high school numbers in mind. Don't let yourself become overwhelmed by standardized test scores. Remember that the numbers colleges list are often the *median* scores, not the cut-off scores. If a school lists its median SAT verbal score as 600, then 50 percent of the class scored higher than 600, and *50 percent scored lower.* Many schools now list the SAT test score range of the *middle fifty percent* of the freshman class. The score range of admitted students is often higher than the range for applicants, but in both cases, there are students with scores above *and below* the given numbers.

Numbers are only part of your application. They will, however, help you determine which schools are, for you, long shots and which are likely to be satisfied with your performance. They will help the admission committee determine if you are a sure accept, a clear deny, or a maybe.

Other sections of the application are less numerical. *Personal Qualities and College Admissions* (College Entrance Examination Board, 1982), Warren Willingham and Hunter Breland's study of applicants to nine different colleges, showed that personal qualities are also a valid indicator of college success; colleges look to the recommendations, essays, and interview to give them a sense of the person. Some colleges, like Hampshire, consider these elements the primary criteria in an evaluation.

Recommendations

Evaluations will be written by your high school counselor and by a few of your teachers. Make them more effective by scheduling an early appointment with your counselor to discuss your college selection. If your high school is large and your relationship with your counselor a bit remote (the national ratio of students to counselors ranges between 140 to 1 and 420 to 1), you might prepare a simple life history or a résumé for your counselor. It's good preparation for filling out the applications and, by listing some of your circumstances and activities, you help your counselor write a specific and informed recommendation.

Approach your teachers early. Ask for recommendations from teachers who like you, for whom you have done well, whose courses relate to your intended area of specialization, and who are themselves articulate, careful, and responsible. You want a positive letter and one that will be consistent with the rest of your application. But don't forget that such a letter isn't likely to be written by even your favorite teacher if he or she is overworked, hassled, and pressed for time. Ask your teachers directly, "Do you have the time to write a strong recommendation letter for me for Bucknell?" Name the school, because that may influence their response. There are students a teacher would happily recommend to a state school who should not expect the same enthusiasm toward an application to Stanford. And don't be downcast if the teacher says he or she is too busy or can't do it. Approach someone else. You don't want your letter gathering dust on the desk of a teacher who *meant* to do it but had too many periods of cafeteria duty to find the time.

You might want to give the teachers your brief résumé. They will rely mostly on what you've done in their classes, but it helps if they know you were entering piano competitions or working nights at McDonald's while you were turning out first-rate reports on Jacksonian democracy. Give the recommending teacher a list of the courses you took with him or her, the grades you received, and any special projects or major papers you did. Students come and go and most teachers appreciate a little memory-jogging. Be sure to provide stamped, addressed envelopes, and fill out all the parts of the form indicated as the student's responsibility. Waive your right of access; it shows confidence in your recommender and adds credibility to the letter.

The Interview

Now for the tricky stuff. The numbers are behind you. What you've done in high school is settled. Don't expend energy or worry over things you can't change: the school you attended, the C + you earned in English II. There are grades to be earned for the senior year and this is certainly no time to coast. But most of the numbers your high school will send to the colleges are fixed. Your recommendations are in the works. The last part of your evaluation will be drawn from an interview and from the essay.

The interview, whether on campus or with a local alumni interviewer, is one chance to present yourself personally to the college. But the interview is usually rather brief and can be intimidating. At one interview, Bernard M. Ravina, a successful applicant to Columbia, was asked, "What do you see when you get up in the morning and look in the mirror?" Ravina reflects: "He was digging for something . . . I was thrown off by the question. He really got on my nerves." Ravina found the best preparation was to go into interviews with a specific sense of what he wanted to emphasize about himself and a set of questions about the school that were not answered in the catalog.

Drafting a résumé may make you comfortable with questions about your academic career and activities. Many of the questions are similar to those asked on the application, so you might want to look over or complete your applications before beginning the interviews. It helps to have one interview at a college that is courting you; you need to feel needed at about this time. Schedule the most important interview late in the sequence; you'll be more experienced and confident.

Do your "homework" and use the interviewer's knowledge of the college to help you get to know the school better. Robert Steadman, accepted at Columbia, Dartmouth, Oberlin, and Yale, advises, "Be ready for anything, but work at making the interview valuable for you. I tried to go into the interviews with an open mind and roll with the punches. But I had questions ready, too. When the alumni interviewer from Yale asked, 'Why Yale?' I asked 'Why do *you* think Yale is the place to apply? What made *you* go there?'" The better your questions, the better the impression you will make and the more useful the interview will be to you. Questions already answered in the catalog waste the interviewer's and your time. Questions about the social life or how many students stay on campus during the weekend are better asked during the campus tour. Make your questions a little aggressive. It's much better to ask "Would you send your child to this school?" than "Do you have a major in computer science?"

The interview is a two-way street, not just an opportunity to impress the admission personnel. Don Heider, college counselor at Cincinnati Country Day, says, "It's the consumer's chance to see where to spend more than $100,000." Use the interview to assess further the fit between you and the school, to learn if you want to choose it.

The interview is not always required and not every school you interview with uses the interview evaluatively. Sometimes you have only half an hour to make an impression and gather information, and the first ten minutes is often spent getting oriented and trying to relax ("Did you find a parking place? How long a drive was it?"). Some interviewers find students too shy or guarded to be accurately assessed in a short, high-pressure meeting. Like the recommendations, the value of the interview may vary. Interviews are becoming less practical with the size and geographic range of most applicant pools. Interviews have been dropped at Stanford and are giving way to mass information sessions at many other schools, such as Brown and Vassar.

The Essay

The essay, however, is still taken as a significant and reliable source of information about the applicant. Gayle Moskowitz, a former guidance counselor and school social worker, says, "The better the college, the more heavily they weigh the essay." A number of colleges—Sarah Lawrence, for example—rank the essay as a primary source of information. For liberal arts majors applying to Northwestern University, it is second only to performance in the high school course program. Some colleges make it optional, or look at it only in "gray zone" cases. Even at the University of Michigan, which receives approximately 25,000 applications, the essay is always read.

Admission committees use the essay to get to know the student in a more reliable, specific, and personal way than the numbers and recommendations provide. Pamela Lazarakis, dean of admission at Gordon College, says, "For us, the essay is a critical component in the application. We're looking for a special commitment and the essay gives us something the numbers don't reveal."

Nancy Siegel, a high school guidance counselor, agrees: "Colleges want a third dimension. Without the essay, the application profile is flat." Even Brigham Young University, with a fairly homogeneous applicant pool, finds diversity in the essays. The university asks applicants why they have chosen Brigham Young; since most applicants are members of the Church of Jesus Christ of Latter-Day Saints, one might expect a fairly uniform response, but as Erland Peterson notes, "Although all our applicants say they want to come to BYU for the education and for the right spiritual atmosphere, this is said in many different ways. The essay can tell us about the thought process, the maturity of thinking, purposes, and goals." The application is a jig-saw puzzle; each part contributes a piece to the overall picture.

What does the essay contribute? Choice is very important here. The process of choosing an answer, and often a question, is central to all college essays. Choice shows something about what and how you think. William Hiss, at Bates College, says, "The essay may help us see and judge the depth of the student's understanding of intellectual or social issues but it also shows the quality and freshness of the applicant's mind." It can show priorities, values, the ability to synthesize and connect, the ability to get something out of an experience.

The essay adds a personal, human element to the application. It can breathe life into your activities, interests, experiences, or family situation, making these elements real and vivid. Nancy Donehower, dean of admission at Reed College, says, "For me the essay is the most important part of the application. For a small college with a personal approach rather than an 'acceptability quotient,' it's the place where the kids can strut their stuff. It tells you a lot about character. It can reveal the person who likes to learn because she likes learning or the person who finds the process greater than the product. It can show how analytical the applicant is. If he says his summer in France taught him to observe cultural differences, and then says, 'For example, in France the cars are a lot smaller,' this gives us a good idea of how little he's thought about and analyzed his life experiences."

The essay can be an explanation of grades or exceptional circumstances in your background. If your grades and scores are not reflective of your ability, if your numbers don't tell all, the essay is your chance to make that clear. (Remember, if there are very special circumstances in your life—an illness, a family situation, a handicap—be sure to tell the college about this. Submit a brief account of this subject whether it's asked for or not.)

The essay also shows what a student will do with an opportunity:

Did she pass it up and use a predictable, prepackaged sentiment?

"I chose Carleton College because Carleton is committed to learning and I want to learn."

Did he take it seriously?

Dartmouth asks you to create an ideal application question and answer it; they do not learn much from responses like "Are you having a nice day?" or "Should this applicant be accepted? YES!!!"

Did she take risks?

"These are the voyages of the Starship Nussbaum."

Did he get Mom to do it for him?

Admission people usually can tell. If they mark the essay "DDI," they've concluded that "Daddy did it."

The essay is particularly useful in determining the fit between the applicant and the college. Success at any school depends on knowing what you're in for; nothing is more bitter than disappointed expectations. Karen Parker, senior associate director of admission at Hampshire, says, "Looking beyond the numbers in a student's application, we want to find students who will develop the imagination and independence necessary to drive their own education. We look to the essay, the interview, and the recommendations for this information." If a college has a particular character—it's progressive or relies on a very special kind of teaching method or curriculum—the essay can reflect your suitability for its special setting: St. John's, West Point, or Colorado College, for example.

Next, the essay shows your writing abilities—organization, analysis, interpretation—and your mastery of the conventions of standard written English. Writing—essays and tests—is important in college.

The University of Vermont requires a school essay in support of its applications; Occidental and Vassar do the same. Other schools encourage applicants to submit writing samples. Since your ability to interpret, analyze, and express yourself clearly, correctly, and vividly will be crucial in most of your college courses, your college essay will be looked at in these terms. Sarah Lawrence rates student writing ability on the basis of the essay, assigning each applicant a 1, 2, or 3. How you write as well as what you write is important to admission.

The essay is particularly important for "gray zone" applications. These folders are often discussed by committees of readers. An exceptional element gives a staffer a basis upon which to defend an applicant's admission. Can an essay get a student in? According to James Montoya, dean of admission and financial aid at Stanford, "Yes, it can. Not a student with a very poor record but it can sway a reader and get an application to the committee for further consideration." At Bates, "The essay can be a powerful 'tipper' in close cases, especially with very strong or very poor essays."

The essay is the part of the application that most effectively personalizes your self-presentation. The recommendations are sometimes questioned, the interview is becoming less common and more of a momentary "snapshot." The essay is the only aspect of the application process that is still open to development and is safely in *your* hands. It is an opportunity to show the admission committee a little about yourself, your insights, your enthusiasm, your writing ability. The essay is also an opportunity to convey, under less pressure and with more preparation than the interview, something of your personal style; it counteracts the numbers and the anonymity of the application process.

The essay fits into the overall pattern of your application. The colleges take it seriously; you should, too. It is part of your need to compete and the college's need to select. If an essay is required or even allowed, use it to present yourself effectively. It is a *separate* part of the application and should convey information not found elsewhere. If you ignore this advice, you defeat the college's purpose in requesting an essay.

Seize this opportunity to stand out from the better numbers, the similar recommendations, the other kids. Don't default on it; don't give it away. It's a wonderful opportunity to speak out for yourself in that dark, dusty room of folders. It's not so terrible and it's not so hard. You've actually done plenty of papers like it already!

A Time Line for Applying to College

Junior Year

1. Visit college fairs, talk to friends and alumni; look at various college guides and ask counselors and teachers for suggestions.
2. Write for catalogs and see what the colleges say they want.
3. Take the PSAT/NMSQT; take SAT II's and Advanced Placement Examinations at the end of appropriate courses of study.
4. Meet with your school counselor and, with your parents, develop a list of colleges of interest.
5. Consider visiting colleges in the spring or over the summer.
6. Mention your plans to the teachers you may want to have write your recommendations.
7. Take the SATs in the spring.
8. Keep a journal or collect interesting "important moment" articles from your reading as samples for your essay.
9. Schedule a strong senior year program.

Senior Year

SEPTEMBER
1. Focus on your classes and achieve the best grades possible in your senior program.
2. Attend college conferences at your high school.
3. Set up campus visits and interviews; attend prospective student days and open houses at colleges of interest.
4. Line up your recommending teachers.
5. Request application packets from colleges that interest you.

OCTOBER

1. Confirm your choices with your counselor.
2. Give recommending teachers the appropriate letters and envelopes. You may want to give them a short résumé. You will definitely want to drop them a thank-you note after the deadlines.
3. Take the SAT I and/or SAT II's.
4. Pool application essay questions by type (see Chapter 4); begin thinking about the questions.
5. Research scholarships that may apply to you; get FAFSA aid forms from your guidance counselor.
6. If applying Early Decision, start writing your application and essay (see Chapter 5).

NOVEMBER

1. Early Decision deadlines are often November 1 or 15.
2. If applying Regular Decision, begin filling out applications and writing essays (see Chapter 5). Your deadlines will fall between December 1 and February 1.
3. You may take the SAT I and/or SAT II's again.

DECEMBER

1. Finish essays and copy them or attach them to your applications. You can download applications from various software (Common Application, ExPAN, College Link) or use the forms the colleges provide.
2. Proofread everything TWICE! Make a checklist to be sure you've had scores sent, enclosed checks, and notified your counselor about each school you're applying to. Mail applications early.

JANUARY-APRIL

1. Follow-up on any missing details.
2. Continue to focus on producing a solid senior record.
3. Continue to visit or interview if you missed a school of interest; it's best to see a college when classes are in session.
4. Prepare and file financial aid forms (FAFSA).

2 What You Know About Essay Writing

A New but Familiar Assignment

When the application packets begin to arrive, the anxiety builds. It was fun looking at the photographs, reading the course offerings, and fantasizing about next fall. But the burden of choice is shifting from the schools you choose to the schools that will choose *you*.

As described in Chapter 1, much of the data for this decision is settled. Grades have been recorded, scores reported, recommendation letters provided. But the essay is yet to be written. The application you're filling out may ask for a list of the items you'd include in a time capsule; or perhaps you've been asked to describe lunch with a famous person. Even a straightforward essay about yourself may seem intimidating; it may seem as if you've never done anything like this before. Your teachers assigned papers and reports, with topics such as the theme of love in a particular novel or the causes of a given war. This may appear to be a very different business.

But think about it for a moment and you'll realize that you have, in fact, done this assignment before—*many* times. All those papers for English class—and for history, and even for science—were essentially like the college essay. And even if the college essay seems harder, it isn't. It's different—and in many ways it's easier.

The Challenge of the College Essay ▬▬

As you have seen in the first chapter, the essay is a special opportunity to introduce yourself. You have an attentive audience that believes this part of your application will give useful additional information, a different and reliable lens on you. And although the admission committee will not choose or reject you on the basis of this single element, the essay can be a strong voice in your favor, a way to stand out from the rest, a determining factor for a "gray zone" application. According to Deborah Wright, dean of admission at Simmons College, "We'll take a risk for the right reason." Sometimes it is the essay that gives them that reason. So while admission people want to hear from your high school counselors and teachers, they also want to hear from *you*.

The college essay should be, in one way or another, an essay of self-analysis. Self-analysis is not easy and it can be especially hard to do at this point in your life, when many of your goals and plans are unsettled. You may already have confronted this problem at the interviews. Admission people ask, "Tell us about yourself" or "What are your hopes and aspirations?" These are questions that require self-analysis, and they're pretty hard. The college has questions about you partly because you still have questions about yourself. But the essay is a chance to demonstrate which questions you've asked yourself and what answers you've found.

The college, then, is asking you to do something genuinely difficult—tell about yourself—and here the pressure is really on. The audience is critical and crucial; readers unknown to you intend to take your performance seriously.

The essay is also going to be examined as a clue to your writing ability. Columbia University lets you know what they're looking for right on the application: "Please remember that we are concerned not only with the substance of your prose but with your writing as well." Andrew Stewart, former assistant director at Hope College, is equally direct: "Of course the essay is seen as an index to student writing. After all, a very large part of your performance and evaluation in college will be based on essays and written tests. Skill in essay writing is essential to success in a competitive liberal arts college. The essay portion of the application is one way to find out if prospective students have one of the basic skills they'll need when they're here." Carol Lunkenheimer, director of undergraduate admissions at Northwestern, sees the essay as a useful defense of a student's acceptability. "It is greatly in an applicant's favor if the reader can say, 'This kid can write.'"

So the challenge is to have your own say with power and precision. *You* in one page! Clearly there is pressure here and it is natural for anything that is challenging to be threatening as well at times. But with yourself as the subject, you actually have all it takes to succeed!

The Structure

A college essay is nothing new; it is the type of writing with which you are most familiar. Let's look at your writing skills and the kind of writing you have learned in the last 12 years.

First of all, it was organized—your paper on *The Great Gatsby* had a format, as did your papers for history and science. They had a beginning, a middle, and an end. You did not just ramble. You focused on a single point and stuck to it, describing and developing your insights and observations. At the end, you returned to your main idea, which you summarized and refocused.

A paragraph on the economic causes of the Civil War might have looked like this:

Beginning: Some of the causes of the Civil War were
    economic
Middle: A sentence or two on Northern prosperity
A sentence or two on Southern agricultural economy
Three or four sentences on the conflicts these
    different economies created in trade, standard of
    living, relations with England
End: A concluding sentence

A paper on *The Great Gatsby* might have been like this:

> Beginning: *The Great Gatsby* explores different kinds
> of love
> Middle:
>   A paragraph about friendship
>   Daisy and Jordan
>   Gatsby and Nick
>   A paragraph about false love
>   Nick and Jordan
>   Myrtle and Tom
>   A paragraph about true love
>   Gatsby and Daisy
> End: Summary/conclusion

A science paper might have looked like this:

> Main idea: Desert animals show a significant
> adaptation to their environment
> Body:
>   A paragraph about adjustment to heat/cold:
>   burrowing animals
>   cold-blooded animals
>   A paragraph about adjustment to weather:
>   natural protections from sandstorms
>   natural protections from dehydration
>   A paragraph about adjustment to limited food:
>   storing nourishment
>   extracting water
> Conclusion: A summary or conclusion drawn from the above

The structure of formal writing has been described in this way:

> Tell 'em what you're gonna tell 'em
> Tell 'em
> Tell 'em what you told 'em

This is a good way to think of your writing. The three parts are a natural way to present any topic. After all, you are leading the reader along an unfamiliar path. You have to give that reader an idea of the basic subject so she can focus her attention. The middle will be meaningful if she's got a focus to follow; she can keep an eye out for love or economic factors. Likewise, with a reiteration or closing comment at the end, you strengthen the coherence of your argument.

You've used this three-part pattern in a variety of situations.

The paragraph	The essay
Topic sentence	Introduction
Development	Body
End sentence	Conclusion

No matter what your writing background, you have worked with this common structural pattern. It has been part of your school curriculum for a number of years and it is something you have practiced. It is a skill that seems to come naturally to most writers when they want to explain something or describe an idea unfamiliar to their readers. Even work on the school newspaper or personal writing may have given you practice in this three-part format:

Dear Joe,
My summer vacation was a blast.
Here is what we did ....
It was really the best.
Love,
Jennifer

You have been taught this structure, and it is just what you need for the college essay. (Sample 1 in Chapter 6 is a good example.) It is also the underlying structure of a lot of college writing, business writing, journal articles, proposals, reports, and speeches. If you're a bit shaky about how it works, pay careful attention to Chapter 3 because you'll need this skill now *and later.*

The Style

You're experienced with the structure you'll need for the essay, and there's more good news: You have also had 12 years of experience with the style. You know the difference between academic and personal writing, between term papers and diaries, between essays and love letters.

Everyone has a natural storehouse of different styles of speech and of writing. You talk to the person taking your order at the local pizza parlor with a very different vocabulary and style than you would use if a corporate receptionist asked, "May I help you?" So you automatically write for each assignment in a different way. Without being conscious of it, you use a style and vocabulary for a paper on *Hamlet* that is nothing like what you'd use in writing a note to Mom. You know you have to check your spelling and you automatically strive for the level of vocabulary and correctness suitable for a finished piece of work.

> Hamlet is like really wacko.
> The guy just can't get over his
> old man's kicking off so he fakes
> being out of it most of the time.

Pretty funny. The humor is a result of mismatching style and situation. Most writers move back and forth between various levels of language and styles of writing as easily as they adapt their speech to their listeners. You know the right level of language for a given situation and you know the college essay is a serious piece of writing. It is also not quite as formal as most school writing; you'll want all the clarity and correctness you can produce but, considering the subject (you), you'll also want a slightly more direct and personal tone than you might otherwise use. Your spelling and sentence structure should be correct but your word choice and style should not be heavily academic, full of thesaurus words, or unnatural for you.

You also have a good idea of what your strengths and weaknesses are as a writer. (If you want more information, look at your writing folder from last semester, or ask your English teacher.) You have plenty of time to proofread, look up potential problem words, and edit your essay. The flow of good ideas is interrupted by dum errers; save time to proofread thoroughly and correct your own dumb errors.

You certainly have adequate motivation built into this situation. It's only a matter of diligence to bring your performance to perfection and, again, you've had 12 years of practice.

The Subject

The greatest strength you bring to this essay has been 17 years or so in the making: YOU. The form and style are very familiar, and best of all, you are the world-class expert on the subject.

You really know a lot about you. If you can write about wars, novels, experiments, and sonnets, writing about yourself should be simple. You don't have to do any research. You don't have to study the major city-states of the Renaissance or read *Macbeth*. You already know all you need to know. And there is a wealth of information, thousands of incidents, events, and facts, from which to draw. Instead of being at a loss for material, you may find the quantity a little overwhelming. However, you don't have to despair of finding a topic; it has been the subject of your close scrutiny every morning since you were tall enough to see into the bathroom mirror.

Another wonderful aspect of this topic is that no one else has it; it is unique. No essay will directly compete with yours. You've picked colleges that are appropriate for you, probably a group of similar schools that include a "long shot" and a "sure thing." They are tailored to you and you are, therefore, tailored to them. Your desires, plans, and abilities probably fall within a profile of each college's student body, so your essay has every reason to stand up to the other submissions.

Remember, the colleges are not looking for a single answer. Admission personnel do not look for a specific student. There is no set combination of items that every applicant must have to gain acceptance at a certain college. You, your essay, and your application profile do not have to match a single narrow standard. They need only fit into one of the constituencies, into the larger pattern of students at your chosen school.

The best part of the college essay is that it can't be *wrong*. One of my students wrote an entire paper on "The Love Song of J. Alfred Prufrock" as if it were a poem set in an aquarium. It turned out she had read the line about the yellow fog and thought it was "the yellow frog" that pressed its nose against the window pane! But had she said she loved aquariums, who could possibly question that? Everyone laughed at the boy who thought "On First Looking into Chapman's Homer" was about baseball, but an essay on his lunch with Don Mattingly would be a different story. Following the advice of Bob Kinnally, dean of admission at Sarah Lawrence College: "Take a deep breath, relax, and believe in yourself." There is no fixed critical opinion about you, no standard theory of interpretation. You can't come off looking bad because you didn't know that Jake's war wound was impotence, that Hamlet's problem was melancholia, that "Stopping by Woods on a Snowy Evening" is about suicide. You don't have to do research. You have had lots of experience with this "text" and you are really the major authority in the field.

The topic may seem hard, but it's really the essay's greatest attraction. It's about you—a topic you know, need to know, want to talk about, have as your exclusive territory, and can't be wrong about. You are the real expert and can easily speak with both authority and conviction.

The Process

Finally, the process of all school papers is the process you will use, and not only as far as the steps to follow. Of course, you will want to brainstorm a little, organize a lot, write, rewrite, and edit; a guide to the composition process is given in Chapter 3. But, the thought process is the same as well: focus and prove.

Let's look back at that paper on *The Great Gatsby*. You chose or were assigned a topic: love. You narrowed it down to a manageable size: three major points. Then you explored the novel and drew out the incidents that proved Fitzgerald portrayed different kinds of love. You gathered as many examples as made your point vivid and then described them to the extent that they supported your theme.

The application of this process to the college essay is simple. In this case, you look into your life, select an element, event, experience, or insight, and assign a meaning to it: that fateful summer, that wonderful biology class, that meaningful job at the ice cream parlor, that exciting lunch I might have had with Charles Darwin. Then you prove the validity of that meaning, backing up and substantiating the view you have taken.

Thus the standard school essay is good preparation for writing a college essay. Academic topics aren't so far from college essay topics. Both are often based on the isolation of a single aspect of some dense and complex phenomenon. A war, a novel, a food chain may be good for a day's lesson. But these are too much for an essay topic, and *so are you*. No teacher has asked you to write on a topic like, "Tell me everything you know about Napoleon"; the college doesn't want to hear *all* about you either. Avoid a sort of shotgun approach; telling everything about yourself is not the idea. Select *one* thing about yourself and illuminate that. The light from one interesting point will reflect a lot about your entire personality. Less is more here. A small and interesting facet will shine most brightly.

The idea is not so much to be different or noble or scholarly. It is better to be vivid and clear. What you want to show is your intensity, enthusiasm, insight, and understanding. This is, after all, what the college wants to see. It's what they hope to measure in the essay and what you'll need to succeed when you're accepted.

Don't panic. You have all the skills you need and the assignment is your best and favorite topic. Your school essays have been your training ground for the right structure, style, and process. The next chapter reviews the process of writing an essay. Chapters 4 and 5 take a look at the college essay questions and present different strategies for making the most of this special essay, an opportunity to introduce yourself to a college.

How To Write an Essay

The purpose of this chapter is to review the process of writing any essay. You may be experienced enough with this form to skim this chapter quickly and go right on to Chapters 4 and 5, which apply the general form to the application essay. Check the summary page at the end of this chapter. If the concepts there seem unfamiliar, or if writing has not been your strength in high school, you will want to read and study this chapter carefully before writing the essays for your applications and again when you begin writing essays in college.

What Exactly Is an Essay?

Essays are as diverse as writers themselves and do not conform to as specific a pattern as sonnets or tragedies or lab reports. However, most essays are some sort of a defense of a writer's opinion or point of view. The opinions vary greatly: Shakespeare's plays all deal with the restoration of order; Springfield ought to build a youth activity center; the United States should no longer invest its tax monies in manned space exploration; gerbils need a stable social environment to flourish; Madonna is the most innovative rock personality around today.

Personal and particular or academic and distant, the essay tries to convince the reader that an opinion, theory, or interpretation is correct. Thus an essay can be a newspaper editorial advocating reduced taxes, a term paper on *The Color Purple* as a tragedy, a proposal from an architectural firm for a shopping mall, or a defense of an innocent client in a court of law. The college essay, too, presents a thesis—a view of the applicant—to the college admission board, and persuades them of its validity. Actually, a great deal of writing involves proving a thesis.

Writing any essay is a process. There are stages and steps to follow. The writer who makes multiple drafts and the one who rarely revises both go through a similar process, either on paper or in their heads. But like Abraham Lincoln, who scribbled a few notes on an envelope on his way to Gettysburg, most writers prefer to complete some of the preliminary steps on paper. The process is:

1. Some preparation and prewriting
2. A number of drafts (from one to several)
3. Some revising and editing

A 45-minute final examination essay in modern European history might involve:

1. Two minutes of preparation
2. Forty minutes on the single draft you will write
3. Three minutes of quick proofreading and revising

The final essay or term paper for the same course would involve:

1. A few days of planning and preparation, with research in the library
2. Two drafts or more
3. Editing and revising; optional review by another reader—a friend, relative, or peer tutor at your school's writing center

The examination essay takes less than an hour; the term paper, one to two weeks. However, the three-part process is used in both writing situations.

> Writing as a Process
> Prewriting
> Drafting
> Editing

Prewriting

The goal of prewriting is to develop your focus; it has four aspects:

1. Brainstorming
2. Grouping and revising
3. Focusing
4. Organizing

Brainstorming

It's time to clean your room. Throw everything that's not nailed down into a heap in the center: books, clothes, albums, letters, used coffee cups, Twinkie wrappers. Now you have a sense of how much you have to do and exactly with what you have to work. Piles can be sorted from the central mess—one for the laundry, one to be saved, one to go in the trash, and so on.

Many writers like to begin with a similar fast and disorganized collection of potential ideas. They throw every possible idea into one place and then look at it. Patterns, groups, and an overall sense of what they have to work with begin to emerge. This is brainstorming.

Take a piece of paper (or work on a computer if you can). Write the limits of your assignment on the top of the page: 750 words on my summer vacation, a paragraph on the importance of the Wagner Act, a 3- to 5-page paper on *Macbeth,* a 10-page paper on Jacksonian democracy and modern populism. Now write down everything you can think of that relates to the topic. List single words that pop into your mind. Ask yourself questions about the topic, make statements, wonder, speculate, recall, and connect. Set a timer or otherwise establish a time limit so that you will keep on writing for several minutes. Do not stop to daydream or reread. Just write, write, write.

Here are two different samples of students' three-minute brainstorms on the film-maker John Hughes:

Sample 1.

> John Hughes: I loved "Sixteen Candles"—he's made a lot of money on "Home Alone"—I loved the little kid and the scene where he puts on aftershave lotion—and the tarantula—and the brother—the parents were mean and didn't really understand the boy—the parents in "Sixteen Candles" forgot about their daughter, too —I liked "Ferris Bueller's Day Off" best.

(This student jotted down a stream-of-consciousness response of facts and personal feelings about the topic.)

Sample 2.

> Makes comedies
> Grew up near Detroit and Chicago
> Went to art school
> Wrote jokes and worked in advertising
> Wrote for *National Lampoon*
> Began doing movie scripts
> First film "National Lampoon's Class Reunion"
> First directing job "The Breakfast Club"
> Likes working with kids, teens
> Lives and films north of Chicago
> Life in a typical suburban town or high school
> Likes being independent
> Best movies: "Ferris Bueller's Day Off" and
>   "Home Alone"
> Uses a lot of sight gags and accidents:
>   "Planes, Trains and Automobiles"
> Likes to show how kids live and feel

(This student is more knowledgeable about the topic; she began with a chronological approach and produced a list of facts rather than a personal response.)

This stream-of-consciousness collecting process can begin without paper and pencil. Some writers mull over an idea for days or weeks or even years. But a significant percentage of writers use a journal, diary, or notebook: They write as a way to begin thinking about writing. Nathaniel Hawthorne, for one, kept such a journal.

> The life of a woman, who, by the old colony law,
> was condemned always to wear the letter A,
> sewed on her garment, in token of her having
> committed adultery.

The beginning of *The Scarlet Letter,* and quite a few other Hawthorne stories, can be traced to the brainstorming he did in this journal. So, for many writing assignments, the way to begin (especially if beginning is difficult and you aren't sure where to begin) is to brainstorm thoughts and responses to the assignment and see exactly with what you have to work. This can be a quick preparation for writing (as for a final examination) or, if you have the luxury of time, you can add to your brainstorm and collect ideas for quite a while before you go on to the next step.

Grouping and Revising

After you have discovered that you do know something about your subject, that you do have a few ideas and questions, go over the brainstorming sheet and look for connections or connectable ideas. You are moving toward a focus. In the second John Hughes brainstorm, for example, there are some film titles, facts about Hughes' life, and various references to comic style.

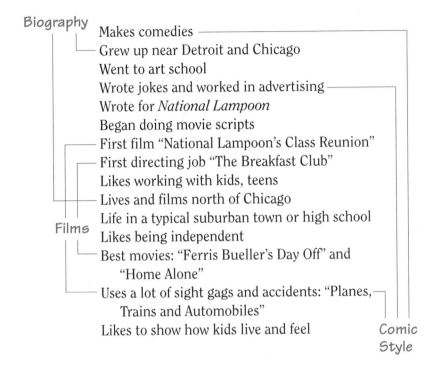

Biography
Makes comedies
Grew up near Detroit and Chicago
Went to art school
Wrote jokes and worked in advertising
Wrote for *National Lampoon*
Began doing movie scripts
First film "National Lampoon's Class Reunion"
First directing job "The Breakfast Club"
Likes working with kids, teens
Lives and films north of Chicago
Life in a typical suburban town or high school
Films   Likes being independent
Best movies: "Ferris Bueller's Day Off" and
   "Home Alone"
Uses a lot of sight gags and accidents: "Planes,
   Trains and Automobiles"
Likes to show how kids live and feel   Comic
                                              Style

Any one of these could lead to a topic and then to a thesis for an essay.

Go over the brainstorm sheet several times, adding any new ideas that come to you. Try to identify more themes or patterns among the items you've listed. Most important, ask yourself questions:

- Why are Hughes' films so popular?
- What makes them funny . . . to kids and to adults?
- Why does Hughes work in Chicago rather than Los Angeles?
- Can comedies be serious, too?
- Are there connecting themes and ideas in all his films?
- Is Hughes a serious film-maker or just a successful one?

What you are doing now is *analyzing* your topic, breaking it down into pieces. John Hughes is too much for an essay; better to concentrate on one element of his popularity, his humor, or his life. An English essay, for example, might focus on one element of a poem: form, language, setting, tone, theme. A history essay on a president might focus on one campaign strategy, one conflict with Congress, one area of impact. A college essay might focus on one job, one experience, one aspect of your personality. Ask questions:

- Why is this important?
- What is the purpose or function of this one element?
- Why did this occur?
- What was the impact of this one event, decision, choice?

All kinds of questions can lead to topics and move you toward a focus and a plan.

Focusing

You need to get down to work now. Your essay must prove a single point or thesis. If this is a 45-minute midterm, latch onto the first topic that jumps off the page and get to the writing as quickly as possible. If this is an out-of-class essay, you need to develop your own thesis. You will shift and adjust this thesis as you work on other parts of your essay, but one angle or aspect of a large and complex topic is your beginning. Look at the groups and clusters of ideas you have come up with and try making statements about some of them.

- John Hughes' films are successful because they appeal to both adults and young audiences.
- John Hughes is essentially a midwestern phenomenon.
- John Hughes' movies show adults as kids often see them: rigid, stupid, and uncaring.

These are preliminary thesis statements and any one of them is a good start: Each focuses on an aspect of John Hughes and asserts an opinion or view about him and his movies.

One interesting sentence can be the basis of a persuasive argument. From the groups of ideas on the brainstorm sheet and the questions you've asked yourself, make your own list of possible thesis statements. If time allows, consult with your teacher or professor about these possible topics. If a full-length research paper is the assignment, a trip to the library's catalog, reader's guides, and indexes in your field might supplement the brainstorming process and help you narrow down and select a topic. Choose the topic that most interests you, the topic about which you have the most to say, the most specific topic you can devise; then get on to the business of making a simple plan.

Organizing

You have chosen a focus; you have a tentative thesis statement. Now you need a plan of attack. You probably are not ready to create a final outline, but it is wise to impose a little order at this point. You need to determine how you will prove your thesis.

Revise your brainstorm sheet and eliminate ideas unrelated to your topic. It may be painful to cross items out, but you can't include everything. A paper that includes *everything* is not an essay; it's still just a brainstorm. Some students write everything they know and hope the teacher will hunt through it and find what he or she wants! Better to prove a small point than require the *reader* to find the meaning in a jumble of information. Take out the red pen and start cutting.

If time and the assignment dictate, you should research your topic. Reread the primary source material, consult critical sources, talk again with your teacher. Begin to line up possible evidence to support your proposed thesis statement.

Once you are satisfied that you have adequate information, rearrange your brainstorm sheet into a tentative list of points or supporting ideas for your topic. Here are three samples of early organizational efforts that include a preliminary thesis and a general plan of proof to be covered in the essay:

Shakespeare's plays deal with the restoration of order

1. *Romeo and Juliet:* the conflict between the Capulets and the Montagues must give way to peace and order
2. *The Taming of the Shrew:* Kate's aggressive attempts to dominate men must yield to a more orderly and peaceful relationship between men and women
3. *Hamlet:* Hamlet's burden is the ghost's command that he restore order by revenging his father's murder

Gerbils need a stable social environment to flourish

1. The control group
   a. eating habits
   b. growth
   c. behavior
   d. mating habits
2. The experimental group
   a. eating habits
   b. growth
   c. behavior
   d. mating habits

John Hughes is critical of adults

1. Parents who are far from ideal
2. Adult criminals or adults who break the law
3. Teachers and school administrators who are boring, nasty, or incompetent
4. Adults who can be tricked by children

As you create a simple outline, choose an appropriate order for your points. One common organizational plan is by time: Discuss a process step by step, the events in a novel in the order in which they happened, the plays of Shakespeare in the order in which they were written.

The most useful order of points in an essay is from least to most important. Remember that the goal of an essay is to persuade. It is therefore logical to begin small and build toward your most convincing argument. When you borrow money from your parents, you mention how responsible you've been recently, your good grades last semester, and other things that set the stage. But your big persuasions—your safe driving record, your plan to fill the car with gas, how desperately you need it—come at the end. You don't start big then fade; you tuck in any tenuous ideas early on and save up for the grand finale.

The same principle applies to writing. The writer of the essay on Hughes looks over the four ideas: parents, criminal adults, teachers, and tricky kids. She decides which she has the most to say about and then revises her ideas, regroups, and builds her argument toward the most persuasive point. The final plan might look something like this:

Thesis: John Hughes appeals to kids by being critical of adults

1. Parents
   a. neglectful parents: "Uncle Buck," "The Breakfast Club," "Weird Science"
   b. parents who forget their kids: "Sixteen Candles," "Home Alone"
   c. demanding parents: "The Breakfast Club," Cameron's father in "Ferris Bueller's Day Off"

2. Criminals
   a. the crooks in "Home Alone"
   b. the parking lot attendants in "Ferris Bueller's Day Off"
   c. Chevy Chase in the Disney park and the Grand Canyon in "National Lampoon Vacation"

3. School personnel
   a. detention monitor in "The Breakfast Club"
   b. "Ferris Bueller's Day Off"
      1) the English teacher
      2) the history teacher
      3) Mr. Rooney
   c. principal in "Uncle Buck"

4. Adults who are tricked by children
   a. Uncle Buck and the oldest girl

   b. "Home Alone"
       1) Kevin with the pizza delivery man
       2) at the supermarket
       3) Kevin and the crooks
   c. "Ferris Bueller's Day Off"
       1) getting Sloane out of school
       2) at the restaurant and in the parade
       3) Ferris's parents
       4) the town, the school, and Ferris's friends

Since there were more examples for the paragraph about tricky kids, an order of importance dictates that this paragraph be last.

This organizing process is not a substitute for the final outline you need for a 15-page research paper; but it is an adequate preparation for most short essays or essay test answers and a necessary first step if such a final outline is required.

Getting the Most Out of Prewriting

The prewriting process can take you from the bewilderment of having just received an assignment to confidence in being ready to write. Use it as much as you need. You may brainstorm and organize a test answer in a total of five minutes, or mull over ideas for weeks, brainstorm three or four times, and then sit down and compose a final outline. Most writers need some help and preparation; they gather their ideas together in a *brainstorm,* sort and *group* them, *focus* on a tentative thesis, and then *organize* their proof in a logical pattern.

Drafting ▬▬▬▬▬▬▬▬

The next step is to begin writing. Complete the research and rereading of sources; continue to refine, add to, and regroup your ideas. Then begin to write your essay in these three parts: introduction, body, conclusion. Although the three parts work together, they need to be thought of separately. The introduction and conclusion are necessary frames for the real substance of your essay, the body. Like the bread in a sandwich, the introduction and conclusion keep everything neat, organized, and together. In between lies the important business, the evidence or proof itself. All three parts make the whole.

The Introduction

There are essentially two strategies for an introduction. One is to provide the reader with a road map for the area about to be covered. This is especially helpful if the territory is tricky or the journey is long, as with a complex or extensive essay. The underlying principle is to provide the reader with a sort of outline of the essay's content.

The Road-Map Introduction

Thesis (main idea)
Reference to each *major* point of the essay
A concluding sentence that returns, in different
    words, to the thesis

Here is an example of this type of introduction for an essay on the novels of Charles Dickens:

> Dickens's novels often present children as the adults or "parents" in their families. In early works like *Nicholas Nickleby,* the real parents are basically unreliable. The children cannot count on them for support, guidance, or love. But the problem intensifies in works like *Bleak House* where adults often act like children. In Dickens's last completed novel, *Our Mutual Friend,* Jenny Wren and Lizzie Hexam suggest the final extension of this theme: they are mothers to their own fathers. Throughout Dickens's works it is the children who run things and hold the families together, while the adults fantasize, dream, or drink.

This introduction does not actually discuss the examples or prove the point of the essay, but it leaves no doubt as to what will be discussed and in what order. It names the thesis, outlines the three supporting points that will be treated (*Nicholas Nickleby, Bleak House,* and *Our Mutual Friend*), and allows the reader to see the general plan of the whole essay.

The General-to-Specific Introduction

The other type of introduction does not outline the paper. Instead, it draws the reader into the topic slowly, leaving the presentation of individual points to the body of the essay:

> A general statement (in the topic area)
> More specific statements that lead to thesis
> Thesis (main idea)

Here is an example of this type of introduction for the same paper on Charles Dickens:

> The nineteenth century took the family seriously.
> Queen Victoria and Prince Albert were a model
> family, the parents of nine children. And in the
> novels that were meant to be read to the family
> group, family connections and relationships were
> major themes. Charles Dickens felt the presence of
> these themes and, as the unhappily married father
> of ten children, knew what family life was like. His
> novels, however, often present the family in a rather
> inverted manner. The children act as parents to
> childish adults.

This introduction slowly defines the areas to be discussed and gradually brings the reader to the topic. The sample begins with the nineteenth century and nineteenth-century families, then goes on to Dickens's own family, and finally to the families in Dickens's novels. The actual novels are not named, but the topic is clearly defined in the last sentence.

This type of introduction is remarkably flexible. It can be brief or lengthy. The opening can be many things; for example, background information, a few words about the author and the time period, begin this essay. (See Sample 2 in Chapter 6 for a college essay that uses this type of introduction.) A definition could also have been used. A science paper on eating habits might want to define "eating" in a broader sense than usual in order to discuss ingestive behaviors in one-celled organisms. This type of introduction could also begin with a common assumption and then contradict it:

> Jobs are scarce. Unemployment is up and people are
> holding on to whatever jobs they have. There's not
> much movement in major corporations and, when
> people retire or depart, their work is absorbed by
> the survivors. Yet this may be the best time in the
> last ten years to look for a new job.

Newspapers and magazines like *Time* and *Newsweek* often use this introduction strategy, capturing the reader's attention with a brief story or incident:

> The hot night of July 26, 1991 threatened a thunderstorm in Henderson, Texas. When Nancy-Jean Alberts went out to empty the trash, she noticed the sky was dark for 8 p.m. and lines of heat lightning darted along the horizon.

This article might turn out to be about a murder, a flood, or even trash. The narration at the beginning has caught the readers' attention and drawn them into the paragraph; a forceful and focused thesis statement will follow.

The general-to-specific introduction is flexible and simple. You have some choices in its construction and do not have to give away all your ideas in the first paragraph. It is suitable for most essays and is especially useful for those in a timed situation when you may not know at the beginning exactly what points (or how many) you will cover. The only pitfall is the first sentence—do not make it overly general. "Life is interesting" doesn't sound very interesting and would require a very lengthy paragraph to narrow it down adequately to a thesis. "Shakespeare is a great playwright" is certainly more specific, but it lacks impact. Don't let the first sentence grab the reader too vigorously, either. An attention-getter is a good idea but it can be overused or overdone. Remember your audience and let it dictate your tone. You don't want to begin:

> Wha-a-a-a-a! Who's that howling in *Bleak House?* Is it a crying baby or is it simply Mr. Skimpole?

Make the first sentence interesting and related to the thesis but try to engage the reader's interest without being confusing or shocking.

Is an Introduction Absolutely Necessary?

Most essays need a paragraph of some length to identify the topic and get things going, but there are a few exceptions. A short essay (one or two paragraphs) does not need an introduction. A few sentences at the beginning of the first paragraph can make the topic clear. Some tests and examinations (and some college application essays) provide only a few minutes or a few inches for your responses. In such a case, a full introduction would waste precious time and space. If you are given an essay test with several questions, do not fret over the introduction for a *15-point* question, "To what extent did Metternich influence diplomacy in the nineteenth century?" Begin with one or two sentences drawn from the question itself (you might simply state that Metternich *did* change diplomatic techniques) and give the rest of the allotted time and space to the *proof.*

Another time to consider omitting the introduction is in an inductive essay. This essay takes the reader through a discussion without a clear focus, revealing its intention only at the end. This is a suspenseful and creative approach to the essay and can be very effective. But, it is best reserved for less stressful situations than the college essay, for the most able writers, and for short, creative topics.

Finally, a narrative essay might survive without an introduction. The writer tells a story, recounts a series of incidents, and then draws meaning from them in the conclusion. Like the inductive essay, this format requires readers to go some distance on faith. They aren't sure to what they ought to be paying attention, but finally, it all makes sense in the conclusion. (Sample 3 in Chapter 6 uses something like this strategy.) This strategy can make a very effective *short* college essay, but remember, it puts a significant burden on the reader and is best reserved for occasional use.

Most of the time, you'll want an introduction and most often either the road-map or the general-to-specific format will give your essay a strong start and a clear direction.

The Body

The substance of your essay is the body. Bound in place by the introduction and the conclusion, the body does the work of the essay: It proves. It presents the evidence that will convert the reader to your opinion. Each paragraph of the body is a block of proof, a chunk of evidence of the validity of your thesis, and each is developed from one aspect or point of your thesis, as sketched out in the simple outline.

The Shakespeare essay, for example, uses three plays as examples to prove that Shakespeare was concerned with the restoration of order. The outline gives three subtopics: order in *Romeo and Juliet*, in *The Taming of the Shrew,* and in *Hamlet.* Thus, you plan three paragraphs for the body, one for each play. If, however, in drafting the essay you discover new aspects of the topic that should be mentioned—perhaps that *Hamlet* is a play about both the proper order in a kingdom and also about one man's drive for personal order and revenge for the death of his father—the plan can be expanded and the number of paragraphs in the body adjusted, in this case, to four, one for each play and two for *Hamlet.*

The important thing is to prove, with specific and vivid detail, the correctness of your view. You must present a sequence of *arguments* for your thesis rather than plot summaries, story outlines, or a review of the course of history thus far.

Selection is the key. You must go through each part of your argument and select the scenes, details, quotations, and facts that show the truth of your view. To substantiate your thesis, you must bring to the reader's attention only that evidence that cumulatively shows that you are correct. Select. Do not retell! It is not persuasive to retell a whole story, review every event of a war, or summarize everything that has been said on your topic. Your essay should be based on your angle of vision, your special lens, your way of looking at a larger complex of ideas. And in support of your thesis, you need to gather *only* those points or ideas that prove your view is right.

Each paragraph of the body should conform to this pattern (or vary from it for a *good* reason):

> TOPIC SENTENCE
> (the main idea of this paragraph and its relation to
>   the thesis)
> DEVELOPMENT
> (the evidence — events, facts, statistics, reasons,
>   examples, details, things said in the literature,
>   things said about the literature—presented in
>   some logical order)
> CLINCHER
> (especially useful in a long or complex paragraph)

Topic Sentences

The topic sentence is important in two ways: it identifies the subject of the paragraph, and it shows how the paragraph is connected to the thesis. It may even form a transition from the previous paragraph.

1. thesis ——— Shakespeare explored the instability of life and the
2. transition ⟍ need for order not only in a comic setting but also
3. topic ⟍ in the tragic circumstances of Prince Hamlet.

1. topic ⟍ But things get worse in *Our Mutual Friend.*
2. transition ⟍ Now parents and adults are not just silly and
3. thesis ⟍ irresponsible; they are the children of the families.

In the first example, the writer reiterates, in slightly different words, the main thesis of the essay, mentions the point of the previous paragraph (a comedy's treatment of this theme), and then establishes what this paragraph will discuss (*Hamlet*). In the second instance, the writer uses two sentences to get going: the first names the paragraph's topic (*Our Mutual Friend*); the second fits that topic into the larger scheme of the thesis (irresponsibility and childish adults).

There is, and always should be, flexibility in a format. Every paragraph does not have to begin with a reference to the preceding paragraph. A topic sentence doesn't have to be first in a paragraph, either. But each sentence that appears before the topic sentence runs the risk of being wasted. Your readers don't yet know what's going on, and may lose interest or the sense of continuity. They ask, "Why am I reading this?" It is therefore helpful if each paragraph declares, and usually the sooner the better, its topic and how it intends to support it.

Development

The middle of each paragraph is the support. It is a combination of facts, events, quotations, examples, and reasons that proves the point of that paragraph and, in so doing, proves the thesis of the essay. It is the evidence that will persuade your reader. Notice the combination of different types of support in this paragraph from an essay about insanity in *Moby Dick:*

Another way Melville makes the reader aware of the transition from sanity to insanity is in his imagery. Throughout the novel, he weaves a careful pattern of images that turn from normal to abnormal, from familiar — Example
to strange. For example, the images of fire begin in the friendly inns of Nantucket and New Bedford. Ishmael rejoices in the privilege of "making my own summer with — Quotation
my own coals" (61). Fire is here warmth and companionship. Even Queequeg's sacrificial fire to Yojo serves — Event
as the beginning of intimate friendship between the two sailors. But slowly this begins to change. By the middle of the novel, fire begins to suggest evil. It is associated with Ahab's mad purpose, what critic Richard Chase in *The American Novel and Its Tradition* calls "the self- — Critic's Opinion
absorption that leads to isolation, madness and suicide" (109). Ahab calls himself a volcano in "The Quarter-Deck" chapter and the crew swears death to Moby Dick in a fiery — Event

Detail crossing of harpoons. Later, in the chapter called "The Tryworks," Ishmael compares the rendering fires to the fires of hell. By Chapter 113, hot-forged harpoons are Event being dipped in blood as Ahab baptizes the crew *"in* Quotation *nomine diabolis"* (373). Nature's fire, lightning, warns Events the crew away by igniting the masts and nearly striking Ahab. The happy homefires of Nantucket have changed into the dangerous fires of Ahab's mad passion; thus they reinforce the novel's movement from sanity to insanity.

Like Melville's imagery, his characters move toward madness. First there is Pip . . . .

Clincher

At the end of this paragraph, a sentence appears that summarizes the whole paragraph and refocuses on the essay's thesis. Because this sentence echoes the topic sentence, a student may wonder if the paper isn't getting repetitious. "Isn't it awfully boring to say this one thing at the beginning and end of the paper, and at the beginning and end of every paragraph, too?" Remember, however, that you are covering ideas familiar and clear only to you. You must make them equally clear to readers who have never thought exactly this way about this topic. They have to be led a little. There has to be repetition. Each topic sentence should sound somewhat alike. Each should relate to the thesis. The concluding sentences of some, or all, of the body paragraphs will return to the main idea of the essay, too. There will be changes in wording and perhaps only the repetition of a key word (like "order" in the Shakespeare essay) to remind readers of what's happening. But don't think you're helping them by retelling the plot. Provide signs, repetitions, along the way to keep readers on *your path*. The end of the paragraph about Moby Dick is a good example of this kind of helpful repetition.

A short or simple paragraph, or one that appears right before the conclusion, does not need the summary sentence at the end. You can draw the paragraph to a close in some other way, perhaps simply by adding a sentence that makes it clear the paragraph is complete.

Remember to follow a logical order in the presentation of the body's paragraphs. Chronological order or order of location have been mentioned as possible types of organization. Another excellent choice is order of importance, beginning with your minor points and building toward your most important argument at the end.

The body of the essay is its most important part. You marshall all the evidence you can find to support your theory and present it in a series of paragraphs designed to convince your readers. Most of these paragraphs will begin with a topic sentence that connects the paragraph to the thesis. All of them will be made up of facts, examples, and extensive specific support for your point. Many will end with the summarizing clincher that redirects the reader's attention to the thesis. The repetitions of the thesis and its rewording in topic sentences and clinchers aren't useless reiterations; they are the necessary coherence that creates the focus. The body should be by far the greatest percentage of the essay for it is there that the essay will win its argument.

Points to Remember

Patterns are useful. Good tailors begin with standard patterns and soon develop their own. So it is with writers. The idea is to begin with rules and use them where appropriate. There is no reason why you can't "break" a rule as long as you have a reason and are doing so consciously. The goal of any writing advice is to help writers be more aware and in control of their material, and to avoid writing with no idea of what they should do or why they are at one point succeeding and at another failing. More than any student comment, "She didn't like my paper" is the one that drives me crazy. I have never graded a paper on whether I liked it or not. I have always determined a grade according to how successful the student was in organizing the material and in validating his or her argument. The paper made its own grade.

Also, keep in mind that there is no secret set of "right" answers stashed in the school safe. The purpose of an essay is not to guess what the teacher believes about a topic and win an A; it is to develop a good thesis and prove it. Critical opinion changes, even among the leaders in a given field. Notice the ups and downs that the reputations of presidents suffer. Consider the esteem with which Hemingway was regarded in the 1950s versus the respect awarded him in the feminist age. To paraphrase Emerson's favorite quotation, "Ask for no man's opinion but your own." Every age must write its own criticism. So the essay is not about latching onto THE ONE RIGHT ANSWER. It is about your ability to find a possible answer and to make a convincing argument for it.

This is especially true for the college essay. Many students set out to "tell them what they want to hear." This is a fruitless and contradictory goal. What the essay should provide is a sense of you, a concrete and specific view with the facts to back it up (prove it).

An interesting idea with no evidence is a pointless exercise in creativity; a lot of plot review or a collection of facts without a focus is merely exposition. Think of two opposing lawyers; each has the same events and facts to work with yet the prosecutor selects and presents them so the accused looks like a cold-blooded murderer while the attorney for the defense selects and presents them so that the client seems as innocent as an angel. Every essay needs a good thesis and a focused selection of supporting material to make it clear and convincing.

Do not wander off this straight and narrow path to either side: to the "let's-tell-'em-what-they-want-to-hear" essay that presents a razzle-dazzle idea with no evidence, or to the "let's-tell-'em-all-we-know-and-hope-for-the-best" (travelog/autobiography) essay that is full of facts with no focus. In any essay (and especially in the college essay), you need both *focus* and *proof.*

A Special Organizational Problem

The Comparative Essay

The comparative essay is a special assignment. It is a challenging format that is often used for Advanced Placement exam questions and final examination topics. The organization is not difficult as long as you keep in mind the comparative purpose of the paper. The pitfall is writing a comparative essay that never does any comparing—lots of information with no comparisons drawn between the points. A history student, for example, asked to compare the programs set up to regulate business that were passed in the administration of Woodrow Wilson with those passed in the administration of Franklin D. Roosevelt, might recount all she knows about Wilson, then all she knows about Roosevelt, and then conclude. This is not a comparison.

One way to get it right is to discuss the first item of the comparison, in this case Wilson's regulatory programs, then discuss the second item in the same order used in the previous paragraph and with *constant reference* to what has *already* been said about Wilson. The second paragraph will include sentences such as the following ones.

> "Roosevelt had opposition similar to that confronted by Wilson, but he employed different tactics to overcome it . . . ," or
> "But like Wilson, Roosevelt found his backers were fickle ....," or
> "These measures finally were more successful than what Wilson accomplished ...."

Proceed in sequence through your points, sticking with the order established in the first paragraph of the body, continually making comparative comments about the similarities and differences of each new point to what has already been discussed. The conclusion for this essay should summarize fully and methodically all the comparisons that you have discussed in the essay.

Another method of organization, more likely to be used in an essay prepared outside of class than for an examination question, separates aspects of the comparison. In the example given above, the writer would isolate individual aspects of the topic—creation of programs, implementation, obstacles, success, impact—and then look at each president's handling of them. Here is a pair of outlines that shows the difference between the two ways of writing a comparison:

A. COMPARING
   WILSON AND FDR
1. Wilson
   a. programs
   b. implementation
   c. obstacles
   d. success
   e. impact
2. FDR (with reference to Wilson)
   a. programs
   b. implementation
   c. obstacles
   d. success
   e. impact
3. Comparative summary

B. COMPARING
   WILSON AND FDR
1. Creation of programs
   a. Wilson
   b. FDR
2. Implementation
   a. Wilson
   b. FDR
3. Obstacles
   a. Wilson
   b. FDR
4. Success
   a. Wilson
   b. FDR
5. Long-term impact
   a. Wilson
   b. FDR
6. Short conclusion
   a. Wilson
   b. FDR

The second way does not necessarily cover more material than the first, but it is more directly comparative and clearly organized. The reader can follow the comparisons more easily, and the conclusion doesn't have to do as much. Like a lot of things in life, the second way is harder . . . but better!

The Conclusion

The conclusion can serve one or two functions. It should refocus the readers' attention on the main idea of the essay, remind them of what they have just read, and reaffirm the validity of the author's argument. This is the summary conclusion and, although not particularly creative, it gets the job done. The format is:

> Thesis (slightly reworded)
> Reference to the major points of the body (in order)
> Clincher

A more creative use of the conclusion is as a springboard for a new idea. After refocusing and briefly summarizing, the writer goes on to judge, speculate, generalize, or recommend.

> Thesis (slightly reworded)
> Short summary of the essay
> Additional idea that grows logically from what has
>   been proven in the essay

This type of conclusion does not suit every topic, as there will be times when you do not have anything to add to the end of your essay. But, there are many times when it can work for you. Here are four examples:

1. The essay on Shakespeare's theme of order might end with a generalization about Elizabethan England and the order that people in that time saw throughout their world. You would thus connect this particular theme from three of Shakespeare's plays to larger trends and ideas of his age.
2. An essay on the athletic facilities at your school in which you urge the creation of an all-weather track might recommend the creation of a capital fund campaign to raise the money needed for the project. The essay itself would only show the need and value of the track. Having reiterated those ideas in the conclusion, you could go on to suggest how the work might get done.

3. An essay on a gerbil experiment might speculate on other possible parallel experiments that could be performed or it might recommend further studies.
4. A college essay describing an applicant might use the conclusion to connect goals and personal qualities to the college itself. For example, if you have proven you are a science buff, in your conclusion you might show why MIT is the logical choice for you. (See Sample 1 in Chapter 6.)

To determine whether this type of conclusion is appropriate, at the end of your essay ask yourself, "So what? What does all that I've proven mean? Where can I go from here?" If there isn't any real answer to this, then sum up and stop. But if a suggestion or generalization comes to mind, you might use it for a "springboard" conclusion. This conclusion is especially useful for assigned essay topics that request the writer to discuss two unequal ideas. For example, a history teacher might ask: "To what extent did the role of women in society change during the 1930s? Do you see any parallels in the situation of women today?" The real heart of this question is the role of women in the 1930s. An additional, although less important, part of the question asks the student to assess his or her life in terms of what he or she has already said about the 1930s. The student constructs an essay with individual paragraphs devoted to areas of change concerning women: the domestic scene, the job market, economic power, fashion. The conclusion might sum up these points and then go on to comment on the writer's own time. Since this is a lesser part of the question, it could be adequately treated as the final aspect of a conclusion. Judgments and comparisons could be based on what has already been said in the body.

This second type of conclusion would not be a good choice if the question asked for the discussion of two *equal* points: "Discuss the forces that created the League of Nations and those that destroyed it." Here, the best bet is a body divided into two sections, one on creation and one on destruction. The conclusion would then merely summarize what was presented in the body.

As you plan and write the essay, you will see how much you have to say, how important are the various parts of the essay, how to structure the paragraphs themselves, how much repetition is needed. You will choose an introduction that suits your topic, create body paragraphs in support of your thesis, and select an appropriate conclusion.

Transition

Everyone who has watched the television program "Wild Kingdom" over the years knows about transition. The host always creates strong transitions between the show and the commercials:

> That lion cub was almost eaten by those jackals. But luckily his father was there to protect him. You'll feel that same security when you're protected by (sponsor's name) insurance.

By repeating a key word (like "protect") and using demonstratives (that, those) and transitional expressions (like "But"), the host establishes a connection between the program and the advertisers.

Transition is the most important stylistic skill you can master. It is the way to create connections and coherence in your writing. It is absolutely essential to a smooth introduction, important within and especially at the beginning of body paragraphs, and helpful as you move into the conclusion.

There are three major ways to create transition:

Rule 1

Use transitional expressions. These words and phrases make connections wherever they appear:

To show time or sequence: first, second, then

To show cause: therefore, thus, hence
To show similarity: and, like, similarly, likewise
To show difference: on the other hand, however
Example: Ahab sees Moby Dick as his goal in life. *Likewise,* Jay
Gatsby sees Daisy as his goal.

Rule 2

Repeat key words and sentence structure (parallelism).

Example: Ahab *sees* Moby Dick as *his goal* in life. Likewise, Jay
Gatsby *sees* Daisy *as his goal.* (Note the repetition of the words
"sees" and "goal" and the use of parallel sentence structure.)

Example: ". . . that government of the *people,* by the *people,* for the
people, shall not perish from the earth." ("People" is repeated in
a series of three prepositional phrases.)

Rule 3

Use pronouns (he, she, it, they) and demonstrative nouns and
adjectives (this, that).

Example: Francis Bacon: He that hath wife and children hath given
hostages to fortune, for *they* are impediments to great
enterprise . . . ."

Example: Franklin D. Roosevelt: "The New Deal is our hope. *It* is
the way to recovery. *It* is the immediate way. *It* is the strongest
assurance that the recovery will endure."

The following paragraph relies heavily on transition to guide the
reader. Notice the different methods used, particularly the paragraph
hook that connects the next paragraph to this one.

Another way Melville makes the reader aware of the transition from sanity to insanity is in his imagery. Throughout the novel, he weaves a careful pattern of images that turn from normal to abnormal, from familiar to strange. For example, the images of fire begin in the friendly inns of Nantucket and New Bedford. Ishmael rejoices in the privilege of "making my own summer with my own coals" (61). Fire is here warmth and companionship. Even Queequeg's sacrificial fire to Yojo serves as the beginning of intimate friendship between the two sailors. But slowly this begins to change. By the middle of the novel, fire begins to suggest evil. It is associated with Ahab's mad purpose, what critic Richard Chase in *The American Novel and Its Tradition* calls "the self-absorption that leads to isolation, madness and suicide" (109). Ahab calls himself a volcano in "The Quarter-Deck" chapter and the crew swears death to Moby Dick in a fiery crossing of harpoons. Later, in the chapter called "The Tryworks," Ishmael compares the rendering fires to the fires of hell. By Chapter 113, hot-forged harpoons are being dipped in blood as Ahab baptizes the crew *"in nomine diabolis"* (373). Nature's fire, lightning, warns the crew away by igniting the masts and nearly striking Ahab. The happy homefires of Nantucket have changed into the dangerous fires of Ahab's mad passion; thus they reinforce the novel's movement from sanity to insanity.

Like Melville's imagery, his characters move toward madness. First there is Pip . . . .

Word Repetition

Transitional Expressions

Pronouns

Paragraph Hook

Try to keep transition in mind as you draft and especially as you revise your essay. It will provide the flow and cohesiveness that every essay needs.

Editing

The final stage of the essay process is editing. Proofread your essay carefully and slowly; read it aloud. Look for:

FOCUS: Check for coherence throughout the essay so that the reader can find the main idea (thesis) and follow it from beginning to end. You might have someone read just your introduction to see what he or she thinks your essay is about. If there's any doubt in the reader's mind, keep rewriting that paragraph. Also be sure your main idea is not only clear in your introduction but is referred to *throughout* the essay, especially at the beginning of body paragraphs.

PROOF: Be sure the development of each body paragraph is extensive, specific, and clearly related to your main point. This is the meat of the sandwich—make it substantial.

CORRECTNESS: Check your spelling (or use a spelling checker on your computer). Even for some very bright people, spelling is always a problem. Find a good dictionary and check every word you're unsure of. Don't be lazy about spelling. I know a recruiter who turned down a good job candidate because he hadn't bothered to spell the company name properly in his application letter. "He's careless; he'll only cause headaches for me and hassles and embarrassment at the top." Right or wrong, we are often judged on small things.

In a second reading, try to pay attention to *how* things are said, as well as to what you have said. Try to read with the eyes of an enemy looking for problems, keeping the following in mind:

1. A simple style is best. Good writing sounds like speech rather than a vocabulary review lesson. Where you are having problems expressing an idea, try using shorter sentences and simpler words rather than longer sentences and a thesaurus.
2. Evaluate your writing for sentence variety. Write some long, complex sentences; use a short sentence once in a while for

impact. Don't begin all your sentences with the subject or with the same word.

3. Remember your audience and the requirements of the assignment. There are differences in the structure, style, and precision required in a science journal and in a finished lab report, in an essay for your drama class and in a final term paper in a Shakespeare seminar for senior English majors only.

4. As in everything, there are usage conventions and somewhat arbitrary rules of formality. Most academic writing requires that you observe these conventions, although each audience will be a little different and each teacher may have his or her own pet peeves. Usually these are explained early in a course or described in the writing handbook recommended by the teacher. In general:

- Avoid dashes and exclamation points. They are the junk food of the punctuation world, just as the semicolon is the truffle. The former are too casual for the tone of most essays; the latter is best used sparingly.

- Avoid parentheses. Most often the sentence merely needs reorganization.

- Avoid asking questions. An essay should answer questions. Asking them is contrived, since you intend to answer them yourself.

- Avoid setting off expressions that are wrong to begin with in sanitizing quotation marks. "Monet was really 'into' water lilies" is not appropriate. Don't try to get away with it by putting "into" in quotation marks. Omit the offending word and state the information in a different way: "Monet found water lilies fascinating."

- Avoid contractions, abbreviations, and slang. Keep your style both reasonably formal and scrupulously correct.

Set the essay aside for a few days—unless it's due tomorrow! If it is, take this moment to resolve *not* to wait until the last minute next time.

When you think you are ready to look at your essay with a fresh, objective eye, go back, reread it, and make any changes that will improve the final draft. Once you are satisfied, it is time for a little outside evaluation. Ask someone whose writing ability you respect to read your essay. The writing center at your school is a good option. Try to pick a reader whose comments aren't threatening to you so you can really hear what he or she is saying. Your boyfriend or girlfriend is probably not the best choice.

Ultimately, you are the best editor. No one can speak for you; your own words and ideas are your best bet. Be sure to proofread the final draft several times yourself to eliminate all errors in spelling, punctuation, and grammar. Errors are distracting and undermine the points you are making, so proofread, proofread, proofread! Spell checking programs aren't enough.

Understanding and Avoiding Plagiarism ▬

You've heard the word *plagiarism* but may not know precisely what it means. Taking someone else's words or ideas and presenting them as your own is a form of stealing called plagiarism. Quotations from *Hamlet* in a paper on *Hamlet* are the support for your theory. Words and ideas from critics who agree with you add credibility to your argument, whether you quote them directly or paraphrase their words. But you must always give credit where credit is due. Identify in the text or by footnotes all direct quotations, paraphrases, and borrowed ideas. It doesn't matter whether the source is today's newspaper, an old out-of-print book, or a friend's research report; you must acknowledge the use of *any* borrowed material.

Reviewing the Process ▬▬▬▬▬▬▬▬▬▬

Summary

The Essay: The written defense of an opinion

The Introduction
    The Road-Map Introduction
        Thesis
        Major Points
        Clincher
    The General-to-Specific Introduction
        A General Statement in the Topic Area
        Increasingly Specific Statements
        Thesis

The Body
    A Sample Body Paragraph
        Topic Sentence (states topic of paragraph, shows relation of
            paragraph to thesis, may show transition from the
            previous paragraph)
        Development (extensive specific examples and evidence to
            support your point . . . about 80 percent of the paragraph)
        Clincher

The Conclusion
    Summary Conclusion
        Thesis
        Major Points
        Clincher
    Speculative Conclusion
        Thesis
        Short Summary of Essay
        New Point (generalization, speculation, judgment,
            recommendation)

The essay process begins with the gathering of ideas by brainstorming, a process which should result in a specific thesis and a simple outline. This can take three minutes during a final examination or several weeks in the preparation of a research paper. Depending on the length and complexity of the topic, you may or may not want to refine and expand the simple outline as you continue to plan, research, and prepare.

Once you're writing, create an introduction that makes your thesis clear. The introduction can also make your whole essay plan clear. The body is the proof, and should be a careful selection of points that validate your thesis. A conclusion at the end should sum up what you've said or raise further possibilities.

Keep your style simple and stress transition between ideas and between paragraphs.

Edit your work yourself and with some outside help. You will probably want to consult a writing handbook for the fine points of style, grammar, research, and footnoting. Check the Suggested Reading list in the back of this book for the names of some helpful reference books. Make a final copy of your essay, proofread it three times, and feel satisfied at having followed a process through from beginning to end.

The essay is a marvelously flexible form. Its only strict requirements are a clear and continual focus and plenty of proof. "Tell 'em what you're gonna tell 'em, tell 'em, tell 'em what you told 'em." Use a beginning to present your thesis, a middle full of persuasive evidence, and an end that returns to and reaffirms the thesis.

Remember that the advice in this chapter is not intended to be an inflexible set of do's and don'ts for writing. These are suggestions, beginnings; some you will always use, some you will outgrow. All are designed to put you in control of your own writing.

What's the Question?

Two roads diverged in a yellow wood,
And sorry I could not travel both
And be one traveler, long I stood
And looked down one as far as I could
To where it bent in the undergrowth;

Then took the other, as just as fair . . . .

from "The Road Not Taken" by Robert Frost

We define ourselves by our choices. The big ones shape our lives: what path to take, what career, who to marry, where to live. But even small choices are self-defining: Do you prefer the top half of the bagel or the bottom? Pepsi or herbal tea? J. D. Salinger or Stephen King? Mac or PC? Colleges believe that by observing the process of choosing, they gain insight into the applicant, so most application essays are experiments in choice. *How* you write the essay will reveal your writing abilities. *What* you write about will reveal you.

Here is a sampling of the application essay policies of a wide variety of colleges and universities—small private and selective institutions and large state colleges. Remember, the small and selective colleges that maintain a more personal admissions process are more likely to require one or two essays. They rate the essay as a major piece in the puzzle. But even large colleges and universities like Brigham Young, Boston University, and Pace University suggest or require an essay, and turn to it for additional insight, in special situations, or to settle "gray zone" applications.

Colleges and Their Questions

COLLEGE OR UNIVERSITY	NUMBER OF ESSAYS REQUIRED	TYPE OF QUESTION	ADDITIONAL SHORT-ANSWER QUESTIONS
Barnard	1	B/C/F	3
Bay Path	opt.	B, J, or M	0
Bennington	1 of 3	B, E, X, or X	0
Bentley	1 of 4	B, X, X, or M	0
Boston Univ.	1	G	0
Bryn Mawr	1 of 3	F, X, or X	2
Carleton	1 of 5	B, C, F, H, or X	2
Case Western	1	G	0
Castleton State	1 of 4	A, C, D, or I	0

NOTE: there are often additional essays for honors programs, special programs, and special scholarships.

A. Tell us about yourself/personal statement
B. Significant experience/achievement/decision/activity
C. Influential person
D. What else do we need to know?
E. Quote
F. Social/political/ethical issue
G. A topic of your own choosing
H. Interview with a past or present person
I. Book, film, or other art form
J. Leadership opportunity
K. Why us/career goals/future plans
L. Predict the future (time capsule, reunion address)
M. Graded academic essay or piece of creative work
X. Other

College or University	Number of Essays Required	Type of Question	Additional Short-Answer Questions
College of Wooster	1 of 3	H, J, or X	0
Columbia	1	G	1
Common Application	1 of 3	B, C, or F	0
Denison	1 of 5	B, B, C, F, or X	1
Dickinson	1 of 4	B, K, L, or X	0
Duke	1 of 4	B, E, G, or X	2
Earlham	1 of 5	E, F, I, M, or X	0
East Stroudsburg	opt.	B	0
Eckerd	1 of 3	B, F, or I	0
Franklin Pierce	0		0
Georgetown	2	A and K	1
Guilford	1; 1 of 3	L; B, F, or X	0
Hiram	1 of 4	B, C, X, or X	0
Hobart Wm. Smith	3 of 3	A, B, and X	0
James Madison	1	A	0
Juniata	1 of 4	B, G, X, or X	0
Kenyon	1	B/F	5
Loyola MD	1	K	0
Mary Washington	2	F and G	0
Maryland Col. Art	1 of 3	A, X, or X	0
Marymount Manhattan	0		1
Moravian	1 of 2	B or M	0
Mt. Union	1	D	0
Niagara	0		0
NJIT	0		1
Northeastern	0		1
Ohio Wesleyan	1 of 3	B, C, or F	1
Pace	opt.	A, F, or M	0

College or University	Number of Essays Required	Type of Question	Additional Short-Answer Questions
Pepperdine	1 of 3	B, F, or L	6
Phila. Col. Pharm.	1	K	0
Radford	0		1
Randolph Macon	1	A	0
Reed	3	K; M; B, H, X, or X	0
Ripon	1 of 2	L or M	0
Roger Williams	1	B	0
Spelman	1 of 4	C, F, J, or X	0
St. John's NY	0		1
St. Lawrence	1 of 3	A, J, or X	1
St.Joseph's	1 of 3	C, K, or L	0
Stockton	1	K	0
SUNY	0		0
Swarthmore	2	B and G	1
Syracuse	1	G	3
Trinity WA	1	M	0
Tulane	1	G	0
Unity	1 of 4	C, D, F, or H	0
Univ. of Chicago	1 of 4	E, G, I, or X	0
Univ. of Denver	1	G	0
Univ. of Maine	0		1
UMass-Amherst	1 of 2	B or X	0
Univ. of San Francisco	1	A/K	0
Univ. of Tampa	1 of 3	B, C, or X	0
Univ. of Vermont	1; 1 of 3	M; B, C, or X	3
Va. Wesleyan	0		2
Virginia Tech	0		0
Wentworth	opt.	B or G	0

The applications have a variety of areas that need more than one-word answers. Not all of these are actually essays. So to begin with, make a list of all the questions you have to answer for your applications. There will be a duplication of questions and you may be able to recycle some of your answers with minimal changes. Schools that accept the Common Application (there are over 164) make life a little easier. And various wordings of the question "Describe yourself" or "Write an essay that gives a sense of you as an individual" appear on many applications.

Don't, however, plan to use the same answer for two entirely different questions. Carol Lunkenheimer, at Northwestern, warns: "We can recognize Stanford's or Dartmouth's question. We want an applicant who cares enough about Northwestern to write an original essay for *our* application." And don't use your answer to "What influenced your decision to apply to Lenoir-Rhyne?" for "Why are you interested in attending Trinity?" There will probably be some similarities in course offerings, programs, location, or philosophy among the colleges you apply to, but the "Why us?" questions need answers tailored to each individual school.

Once you've sketched out what you have to do, you can see that your answers will vary in length. Some questions provide an inch or two for the answer; some give a full page with the offer of additional sheets if needed. Stick as closely as possible to the space provided. The college is suggesting how extensive and complex an answer they want by how much paper they supply. Let that be your guideline. Don't fall too short or go much beyond the limit. Readers are assigned many folders to evaluate and are not perusing your application at their leisure. Make your answers *very legible* and to the point. In all likelihood, three or four pages in a crabbed, bunched-up scribble will be skimmed; you'll get more attention with a concise, typed performance.

Short-Answer Questions

The real difference between the questions is the issue of choice. Some questions ask for a simple list of activities, summer work, jobs, honors, or recent reading. These questions are not difficult and do not require soul-searching. Some schools even ask for this information in the form of a chart. The simple résumé you created for your guidance counselor or your recommending teacher will help with these descriptive questions.

As a List

List the items chronologically from most recent to most remote, or from most important to least. Provide complete information and follow the same format for each item:

June-August 1996   Lifeguard
Springfield Town Pool
40 hours per week
$7.00 per hour

June-August 1995   Swimming instructor
Springfield Day Camp
20 hours per week
$8.00 per hour

In Paragraph Form

Include the activity, your involvement, and the time commitment. Be sure to clarify names of groups or titles since *The Mirror* or Key Club by themselves are not clear to admissions personnel. As one admissions staffer put it, "At some schools the Spanish Club is just a bunch of kids who get together on Friday nights for tacos." Make it clear that your activities have involved responsibility and effort.

1. I am now president of the Book Worms, a school club that does volunteer work for the town library. Each month I attend one two-hour planning meeting with the library staff and schedule

time slots and assignments for the 11 other club members; I work at the reference desk from 7 to 9 p.m. every Tuesday night.

2. During my junior year, I was assistant sports editor for *The Mirror,* our monthly school newspaper. I wrote at least one story for each monthly issue and edited one or two articles by the junior high sportswriter for each issue.

Don't list minor involvements, jobs you held for a week, or a book you meant to read but didn't. A list of impressive activities that you know nothing about and have done nothing more than sign up for is worthless and dishonest. The student who founded the Nuclear Awareness Club in May of his junior year and now lists himself as president is clearly not so much interested in nuclear awareness as in nice-looking credentials on his application. And the less said the better about the girl who listed her two favorite books as *Canterberry [sic] Tales* and *Wuthering Heights* by Jane Eyre. These questions ask for simple, matter-of-fact answers about what has interested you and engaged your time; be complete, clear, and, above all, honest.

The Real Essays

If the application asks you to select *one* activity, achievement, or experience and discuss what it means to you, the question requires a response, whether short or long, that is not simply factual—it requires choice. These are the tough ones. They come in three varieties:

The "You" Question

Most of these boil down to "tell us about yourself." Some examples:

1. A personal statement

"Please complete a one-page personal statement and submit it with your application." (James Madison University))

"Write an essay which conveys to the reader a sense of who you are." (Columbia University)

"Please write a personal essay, telling the Admission Committee more about yourself. This essay . . . is your opportunity to speak in your own voice about something that matters to you. The choice of topic is entirely up to you." (Syracuse University)

2. Describe a significant experience, interest, challenge, or value.

"Tell us about one of the best conversations you've ever had." (Pitzer College)

"Evaluate a significant experience or achievement that has special meaning to you." (Common Application)

"Describe any interesting experience you have had during your college admission search." (Juniata College)

"Creative people state that taking risks often promotes important discoveries in their lives or their work. Discuss a risk that has led to a significant change (positive or negative) in your personal or intellectual life." (Simmons College)

"Describe the most challenging obstacle you have had to overcome; discuss its impact, and tell what you have learned from the experience." (Guilford College)

3. How have you grown and developed?

"To learn to think is to learn to question. Discuss a matter you once thought you knew "for sure," that you have since learned to question." (Bryn Mawr College)

"How would you describe yourself as a human being? What quality do you like best in yourself and what do you like least? What quality would you most like to see flourish and which would you like to see wither?" (Bates College)

The "Why Us?" Question

These questions focus on your choice of school or career as self-reflective. Some examples:

4. Why have you selected College X?

"Why is UVM a good college choice for you?" (University of Vermont)

"Tell us about yourself, your reasons for applying to USF, and your reasons for seeking a college education." (University of San Francisco)

"Describe your reasons for selecting Loyola College and your personal and professional goals and plans for after college." (Loyola College MD)

5. Why have you chosen this program or profession?

"Please tell us about your career goals and any plans you may have for graduate study." (Westfield State College)

"We would like to know . . . what experiences have led you to select your professional field and objective." (Boston University)

"Please relate your interest in studying at Georgetown University to your future goals." (Georgetown University)

The Creative Question

6. The issue question

"Do you believe there is a generation gap? Describe the differences between your generation and others." (Denison College)

"Discuss some issue of personal, local, national, or international concern and its importance to you." (Common Application)

"In your opinion, what is the greatest challenge that your generation will face? What ideas do you have for dealing with this issue?" (College of the Holy Cross)

"What is the value and importance of community service in our society and tell us what it means to you." (Ohio Wesleyan University)

7. The hero or influential person question.

"Who do you feel has served as the strongest Afro-American role model in this century and why?" (Spelman College)

"Indicate a person who has had a significant influence on you, and describe that influence." (Common Application)

8. The book question.

"Choose a significant book, piece of writing, or research article that you have read in the past year. Explain the author's thesis and discuss how she or he proves or argues that thesis. Explain why you think the work is significant." (Earlham College)

"Discuss some creative work that could serve as a key to the way you see the world and the way you see yourself in the world. The creative work may be a scientific theory, a novel, film, poem, song, or any other art form." (University of Chicago)

9. A quotation to comment on.

"John Keats said, 'Even a proverb is no proverb to you till your Life has illustrated it.' Please tell us about an experience in your own life which illustrated a proverb, maxim, or quote that has special meaning for you." (Duke University)

"'Lying is done with words and also with silence.'—Adrienne Rich" (Connecticut College)

10. Imagining the future

"How can I prepare educationally for the 21st century?" (Hampton College)

"You have just completed your 300-page autobiography. Please submit page 217." (University of Pennsylvania)

"For some prognosticators the end of the world was in sight by the year 1000. How do you foresee your world of 2020." (Dickinson College).

11. An academic essay or school paper.

"In lieu of an essay, Lehigh requires each applicant to submit a graded writing sample of reasonable length in any subject . . ." (Lehigh University)

"Please submit a copy of a graded writing sample which you believe will assist us in evaluation your application." (Trinity College DC)

12. Others.

"Ask and answer the one important question which you wish we had asked." (Carleton College)

"Reflect on the relationship between passion and compassion." (Bennington College)

"What is the biggest misconception people have of you and why?" (Hiram College)

"If you were given the money to start your own business, what business would you choose and why?" (Bentley College)

"Write your own recommendation for admission . . . " (Hobart and William Smith Colleges)

"What else do we need to know?" (Unity College)

". . . a story, play, or dialogue that meets all of the following requirements.
1. You must begin with the sentence, 'Many years later, he remembered his first experience with ice.'
2. All five senses—sight, hearing, taste, touch, and smell—have to figure in the plot.
3. You have to mention the University of Chicago, but, please, no accounts of an erstwhile high school student applying to the University—this is fiction, not autobiography.
4. These items must be included: a new pair of socks, a historical landmark, a spork (the combination spoon and fork frequently seen among airline flatware), a domesticated animal, and the complete works of William Shakespeare. Have fun, and try to keep your brilliance and wit to three pages max." (University of Chicago)

. . . and there are more.

Underlying all these questions is choice. The question may be direct and ask you to choose something about yourself to discuss, or it may be indirect and require you to write about something either relevant or tangential to the admissions process. Some schools ask you to explain why you chose them or why you chose college at all. Others like a less relevant go-between: choose an event, person, book, quotation, woman of the year, photograph, or invention. You may have to choose a topic; you will certainly have to choose and limit what you include in your response.

Why is the process of choice a significant source of information about the applicant? Why do so many colleges believe they will learn about you—and some think they can learn the most about you—by observing the choices you make? (Note that interviewers employ this technique, too: "If you were a color, what color would you be?"

"Whom do you admire most?") First, choosing shows *preferences*. Personality assessments and tests like the Myers Briggs Type Indicator use preferences to draw conclusions about character, personality, and counseling. Are you an arts person or a hard-facts science type? Certainly, there is a difference between the person who would like to talk to Machiavelli about the cold war and someone who would share a tuna-fish sandwich with Isolde to find out what it's like to be the object of a great and doomed passion. The choice would be revealing.

Second, choice also reflects *values*. The person who drives a tomato red 1971 Volkswagen until rust leaves nothing for the floorboards to cling to is making a statement about how he wants to spend his money and what he cares about. We say, "That dress isn't me" or "I'm not a cat person." In choosing, you indicate what matters to you and how you perceive yourself.

Third, choosing shows *how* you think. Are you whimsical, a person who chooses on impulse? Or are you methodical, careful, a person who gathers background information before choosing? Questions about you and about career and college reflect these choosing patterns, and even a question about a national issue can show your particular *thinking style, level of intelligence, and insight*. The process, too, is under scrutiny here—how carefully the question has been considered, how extensive is your knowledge, how seriously you regarded the choice.

Do you analyze and think about things that happen to you? Do you feel most comfortable discussing recognized issues, writing about AIDS, South Africa, war in the Middle East? Are you a risk taker, writing an essay that makes a case for itself out of missing socks, lunch with A. A. Milne, the heroic qualities of Jim Henson? Do you respond with a direct answer or go wordy and pompous: "One concept that I've been concerned with recently is reality."

The college regards your choices as a way to evaluate your preferences, values, mental processes, creativity, sense of humor, and depth of knowledge. The writing itself reflects your power of persuasion, organizational abilities, style, and mastery of standard written English. You can see why so many colleges want an essay and why admissions personnel read folder after folder. It's a very fruitful piece of the puzzle. Ten aspects in 500 words! The essay is worth your serious attention. Give it all you've got. IT MATTERS!

The Questions

The goal of all three types of questions is the same: to gather more, and more personal, pieces of the jigsaw puzzle of you for the admissions office to consider. Since the goal is the same—to get you to reveal yourself through your choice—the strategy is the same for handling what seems like, but is not, an incredible diversity of questions.

A Closer Look at the "You" Question

Many colleges ask for an essay specifically about you.

"In what ways have you grown intellectually during your years in high school?"

"Evaluate a significant experience or achievement that has special meaning for you.

"You are strongly encouraged to use the space provided below to describe yourself, your previous academic performance and general interests.

"There are limitations to what grades, scores, and recommendations can tell us about any candidate. Please use the space on the back of this page to let us know something about you that we might not learn from the rest of your application."

"This is your opportunity to tell us about yourself. What would you most like the Admissions Committee to know about you in reading your application."

These questions boil down to "Tell us about yourself," a query you enjoyed answering when you had to devise a yearbook quotation. You weren't intimidated then, and don't be now! The school just wants to know you better and see how you'll introduce yourself.

Advantages of This Question

1. It is direct. The college is asking you to add a clearer sense of you to your application. Remember, it's your best subject!
2. It is an open opportunity to speak for yourself, to plead your own case. If this is where you want to go to school, now is the time to put all you've got into letting them know that you're a "must admit" candidate. Your essay should reveal your personality, warmth, insight, and commitment.

Dangers of This Question

1. It is extremely open-ended. Remember that selection is the key. Find just one or two things that will reveal your best qualities.

Focus is very important. (Use the essay process described in Chapter 5 to get a good focus.)

2. There is a temptation to default and tell everything, rather than focus on a single, illuminating point. Beware of the unedited autobiography.

3. Tone: You may feel self-conscious but you don't want to sound distant and academic. Some students use their stuffiest style and forget this is a personal essay. They think they ought to sound scholarly and write essays full of sentences like:

> "Multitudinous *homo sapiens* in our contemporary culture are so engrossed in the trivia of material acquisition and success that they lose their intimate relationships with the essential elements of life love, learning, and liberty. I myself am not one of those people."

Capitalize on the directness of this question and avoid the pitfalls. Look at yourself as a text, brainstorm and select an interpretation—one focus, one view of yourself—to send to the college. Then back it up with real and vivid events from your life that *prove* the interpretation you've chosen. Several strategies for doing this appear in Chapter 5.

Exploring the "Why Us?" Question

Some schools ask for an essay about your choice of a school or particular career.

"What influenced your decision to apply to NJIT?"

"Why have you chosen to apply to Simmons College?"

"Please relate your interest in studying at Georgetown University to your future goals. How do these thoughts relate to your choice of major?"

"Assess your reasons for wanting to attend college. How have your previous experiences influenced your current academic and/or career plans?"

They are looking for information about your educational direction and career goals. They also want to get an idea of how much you know about them, what research you've put into your choice process, and how serious your commitment is to this particular school

Advantages of This Question

1. It is directly about you, an area in which you have great expertise.
2. You will not have difficulty finding something to write about. You have already been through the business of selecting schools and choosing X over Y; your reasons and choices are familiar and settled.
3. The focus is provided: why you chose the school. The proof is right in the catalog.
4. It is very important to understand where you're going and why. Bennington's study of successful students found that intelligence, emotional stability, and *a solid knowledge of Bennington and its philosophy* made their students succeed. Clearly, the information used in your answer is as important to you as it is to your application.

Dangers of This Question

1. You might not know your subject thoroughly enough. If you've chosen New York University because you want to be close to urban night life, this says something about your academic commitment. If you're going to Smith to major in dance, the school can tell how carefully you've chosen (Smith doesn't have a dance major).
2. Again, tone can be a problem. You want to be neither arrogant nor self-effacing. Rather than trying to flatter the reader, show a concrete knowledge of the school. Bernard Ravina, a successful applicant to Columbia, cautions, "Don't compliment the school outrageously . . . snivelling is not good for you and it is not good for the impression you are trying to create." Nancy Donehower,

dean of admission at Reed, complains, "Too many kids give us an ingratiating answer drawn from the catalog. It's insincere and it doesn't fool anybody."

Know the college and say, in a matter-of-fact way, why it is the one for you. This is your focus. Don't forget the proof, your specific and factual knowledge of the college's programs and special advantages. Name names, course offerings, professors, facilities. Make a clear and vivid connection between you and the school. Chapter 5 offers two strategies for dealing with this question.

Understanding the Creative Question

The last kind of question provides a more creative outlet for your response. Instead of trying to get a look at you through your choice of school, the colleges that use this question try to evaluate you through your choice of some tangential item: a national issue, a famous person, what you would put in a time capsule, a photograph.

"If you could travel through time and interview a prominent figure in the arts, politics, religion, or science, for example, whom would you choose and why?"

"Tell us about a teacher who has had a significant impact on your intellectual growth. How?"

"Of all the books you have read, which has made the deepest impression on you? Why?"

"Ask and answer the one important question that you wish we had asked."

"Please attach a photograph of something that has special meaning for you. Explain your choice."

"Explain why a particular day in the recent past continues to be important to you."

This, too, is an essay about you. The school is looking at your creativity and the breadth of your knowledge and education. They may find out if you read the papers, or just listen to five minutes of news when your favorite rock station takes a break. They may find out what you've read and how much you've thought about it. They may also find out if you can put yourself into an imaginary situation.

Advantages of This Question

1. A focus is provided. The range of your answer is somewhat limited by the question's designation of a hero, book, or national issue. You have something to react to.
2. The creative part of this question can help you with your proof, the evidence of the "you" that you're sending them. This is actually not such a hard question because the proof is easy to find once you've chosen your focus.
3. It can actually be fun! Your focus is you as an artist? Send a photo of your work or have lunch with Renoir. Your focus is the creative you? Send an X-ray of yourself or nominate Robin Williams as man of the year.

Dangers of This Question

1. *The essay without substance.* Some seniors forget the importance of substantiation and write an uninformed essay. Don't write about lunch with a famous writer and get the titles of his or her novels wrong. Don't nominate Desmond Tutu as man of the year if you haven't been following the politics of Africa. Research, as with the choice of school, can make a difference.

   In general, watch out for the national and international issues questions; it's very hard to be well informed. There's nothing wrong with an essay on South Africa or world hunger, if these are true concerns of yours. The rest of your application will support your choice. The problem is the insincere and therefore vague essay. Don't try to write "what they want to hear." Write about your real concerns; it's more revealing and a lot easier. A general and predictable piece of noble prose is a wasted effort if it lacks substance.

2. *The essay without sense.* Some seniors forget their purpose and write a crazy essay. Doubtless, truly creative essays can be very effective since popular topics are "safe" and therefore a little boring. Some admissions personnel, like Carol Lunkenheimer at Northwestern, say they would like to read "more quirky essays." Don Heider, at Cincinnati Country Day, thinks, "A risk is worth it for the 'reach' school."

Taking risks is a good idea but let common sense (and a few editors, readers, friends) be your guide. Admissions personnel may complain about too many "safe" essays, but risk essays can backfire. Vulgarity is never a good idea and eccentricity can be dangerous. Some essays have stuck in readers' minds so tenaciously that they were unable to form a balanced judgment of the applicant's strengths. A fine applicant to an Ivy League school began his essay, "I am a racist, a sexist, and a bigot." It was hard to imagine why that essay was there; it was hard to forget. His high school record was memorable; his application was rejected.

The creative element is a problem for many students. They forget everything they know about writing and stray off the path by neglecting substance or sense.

We are not all creative souls. Few seventeen-year-olds can write like Russell Baker or Dave Barry. Few adults can! The eccentric essay is a real challenge and a risk; don't rush to that option too quickly. It's a gamble that could pay off . . . or bankrupt you.

Counselors may steer you away from certain topics. Remember Yale's instructions: "In the past, candidates have used this space in great variety of ways . . . There is no 'correct' way to respond to this essay request. . . ." No answer is wrong—but sloppy, general, insincere, or tasteless responses hurt. The travelog, the national or international issue, and autobiography may be problems because they are too extensive and therefore too general. But some of the best essays, the memorable and unusual ones, are about very similar, *just more focused,* topics.

Essays about your family, football team, trip to France, parents' divorce, or twin can be effective as long as they're focused and specific: a single Christmas Eve church service, a meal of boiled tongue in Grenoble, dipping ice cream on a summer job. The best essay I ever read, whose author went to Yale then to Oxford on a Rhodes scholarship and then to a Wall Street brokerage house, was about the author's experience on the football team.

The point is NO LEGITIMATE TOPIC IS WRONG! Use your head, be sincere, and treat anything you write about with specifics and focus. Chapter 5 suggests some different approaches for all of these questions.

Other Essay Problems

What if they give me only two inches in which to answer?

Some colleges, like Bryn Mawr, Northwestern, Pitzer, Radford, St. Lawrence, and Reed allow only a paragraph for your answer to one of these questions. Others ask for an essay on one topic and designate other topics for paragraph answers. These questions are mini-essays and should be approached with the same care and attention you gave to the Big Essay. The colleges are asking you to do the same work as other schools only to condense it all into an inch or two instead of a page or a page and a half. Use the paragraph format discussed in Chapter 3. The process, however, is the same as that described in Chapter 5. Just reduce the introduction and conclusion to a sentence each. Try to make your topic vivid in a few lines—and never sacrifice specifics.

The principle is the same, regardless of the length of your answer. You may even want to write 500 words in response to these questions and then cut to the core, to the best 100 words, so only the most direct and clearest point is left.

What kind of writing sample should I send?

Some schools require or encourage submission of an academic essay or writing sample. There is no reason not to send a school essay. As you saw in Chapter 3, a lot of college writing is similar to what is done in high school. Choose a strong performance (a B + or better) and a paper on a not-too-esoteric topic. Do not send a 15-page term paper or a collation of library research. A short, illuminating essay on one poem, one lab experiment, one incident in history, is a good choice. Have a little consideration for your reader and send the original (if your handwriting is good), a typed copy (if it's not), or a high-quality photocopy. And try to send a paper with a fair number of teacher comments. These show how hard you've worked and how demanding your teachers have been. Poetry and creative writing are options also. But most high school seniors do not have enough writing experience to produce first-rate poetry and fiction. Unless you've won an award or received some other type of outside encouragement for your work, stick with a good expository essay of three to five pages.

Summary

There are many kinds of applications but essentially only three types of questions, all of which are meant to reveal how you choose. The key to success for all of them is to choose a clear *focus* and then *prove* your choice. If you can persuade your readers, you have won the day. Prove you're a creative person, prove you belong at the college to which you're applying, prove that the world needs a better mousetrap. The proof is the key.

Also, remember that although the essay should reveal information not found elsewhere in the application, it is part of a larger pattern emerging from your application. The essay about M. Lapardieu, who shaped your life and made French exciting, may not seem very original, but it will connect to straight A's in Advanced Placement French and a teacher recommendation from the head of the language department. Your choice of Georgetown and your plans for a career in nursing will be corroborated by good grades in science and work at the local hospital. An essay on the space shuttle in an application with nothing else about astrophysics or the sciences may raise more questions than it answers. It is the proof that makes a choice valid, worthwhile, insightful. Only the essays with a clear focus and specific proof convey the best *you* to the admissions committee.

5 Focusing on You

Contrasting Two Essays

Essay 1

Throughout my high school years, there have been many factors which have influenced my interests and personality. Being a well-rounded student, I have had many experiences working with people as well as with books. I have learned a great deal through these experiences.

A major influence in my life has been my family. Their love and encouragement have motivated me to expand in many areas of interest.

Another factor which has influenced me is my involvement in many activities outside of academics. Working with my peers in musicals, tennis, dance class, volunteer work and various committee and staff work, I have gained a sense of achievement and accomplishment. I have learned to work better with people, learning the value of team effort. I have gained an appreciation for the talent and hard work contributed by each and every person concerned with the project.

Working in Maine during the past few summers, I have learned much about dealing with people in a great variety of situations. My co-employees, being older than I am, also helped me to mature and accept things as they are. Furthermore, I now know more about the economic aspect of life, both business and personal.

In college, I plan to continue to live a well-rounded life, meeting and working with people from a variety of backgrounds. I expect to prepare for a profession that permits me to be closely related to children as well as adults. I want to help people. I have gotten so much out of life through the love and guidance of my family, I feel that many individuals have not been as fortunate; therefore, I would like to expand the lives of others.

I am excited about the possibility of attending [College X] I feel that I am ready for college. I am ready to accept the challenge of the academics. I plan to give my best to [College X], knowing that [College X] will do the same for me.

This is the kind of essay admissions personnel read all day long. It is not, however, the kind of essay they remember, nor the kind that sends a "gray zone" application to the committee for reconsideration. At a highly competitive school, it's the kind of essay that might be classified D.O.A. (dead on arrival). Most important of all, this is not the kind of essay you want to write.

William Hiss, at Bates, calls these "Boy Scout" essays. They describe an ideal student—eager, involved, loyal, thrifty, reverent—but it's a general picture, not a real person. The college can't make use of this kind of picture. (In fact, in 1982, Yale changed its essay question, hoping to broaden the range of responses and reduce the number of predictable or "safe" essays they received. The University of Chicago's questions are in part motivated by the same intention.) This essay does not *add* to the application because it is unfocused and too general; it could apply to any high school senior. Okay, you didn't summer in Maine. Make that California or any place in between. And you were more interested in lacrosse and the yearbook than tennis, dance, and the school musicals. Change the college's name to the school of your choice and you're all set. Three changes. Whatever else this essay has going for it, it can't do much for the author if three changes could make it yours. It wastes the opportunity to convey to the admissions committee a fresh and vital sense of the writer.

Essay 2

Someday, I hope to have a career in the biological sciences. I've always enjoyed the study of science, with its plausible explanations for the 'hows' and 'whys' of our lives. My serious interest in the area of the sciences developed in my sophomore year, during which I took Advanced Placement biology. One aspect of that course I particularly enjoyed was the final project of designing, conducting, and writing up my own experiment.

Although the work involved was time-consuming, doing the experiment allowed me to see how real scientists test hypotheses. My laboratory dealt with the effects of photoperiod and temperature on the growth of zea mays seedlings. Not only did I have to care for and daily alter the photoperiods of the plants, I also had to measure, every other day, the heights of 76 corn seedlings. As the labs were to be researched and prepared on a college level, I spent several hours in the library at Washington University and Meramec College, using the *Biological Abstracts* to find information on experiments similar to my own which had been written up in scientific journals. The effort required by the lab really made me appreciate the scientists who spend their lives proving or disproving theories by experimentation and research.

Ironically, the experiment was personally rewarding because my original theory was actually disproved. I hypothesized that the plants with the longest photoperiod would grow the fastest. After I concluded the lab and began analyzing the data, however, I found that the plants with a *median* photoperiod grew faster. I thought that this was very exciting; potentially routine results were given a twist.

I consider my biology experiment to be a valuable scientific experience; I was exposed to the methods and materials of *bona fide* scientists, and, in a small way, felt the excitement of discovery. That laboratory intensified my interest in science. Last year, in chemistry, I conducted more self-designed experiments, including one to test the amount of copper in copper chloride, and another to determine the amount of oxygen required for survival by a fish, a mussel, and a clam. These experiments were also worthwhile, but I still consider the *zea mays* experiment to be the most exciting lab I've ever done.

A sense of this girl—her way of looking at the world, her involvement and enthusiasm—comes across. Unless you took Advanced Placement biology, did a corn experiment, read *Biological Abstracts,* learned about scientific research, and made connections between your work in that class, other classes, and your career plans, you couldn't write this particular essay. Its strengths are its clear focus (the Advanced Placement experiment) and its specifics (the class, the 76 seedlings, *Biological Abstracts,* Meramec, copper chloride, the clam). These make it memorable and unique. According to Margit Dahl, director of admissions at Yale,

"We want a strong and well-developed personal point of view, not an institutional response." The *focus* and *proof* are what make this essay. In Essay 1, the writer assures us that her family is supportive, that she learned a lot in Maine, and that she wants to help people. But there's no evidence of any of that. In Essay 2, the writer *shows* her points. She says she enjoyed the study of science and the 76 seedlings prove it.

Most college essays fail on one of these counts: They're either too comprehensive (no focus) or too general (no proof). Those with no focus are the autobiographies and the travelogs; those with no proof are the "Boy Scout" essays. Regardless of which essays you have to write, you want them to be personal, to be distinctively yours; to accomplish this, you must write focused and specific responses.

Prewriting: Creating a Self-Outline

Step 1: Brainstorm

Begin with YOU. As explained in Chapter 4, the questions are all attempts to learn about you. Follow the basic writing process reviewed in Chapter 3: prewrite, draft, edit. These steps are as useful for a college application essay as they are for an English paper on *Hamlet*. The text just happens to be you. So begin with you.

Start by brainstorming. Sit down with paper and pencil and fill a page with statements about yourself. List things you've done, places you've been, accomplishments you're proud of. Set a timer or a time limit and write until the page is full. Write down everything you can think of about yourself: the good, the bad, the special, the obvious, the habitual, the extraordinary. Don't consider your audience at this point. This performance is just for you.

If you have followed the plan in Chapter 1, you have plenty of time. Keep a journal for a few weeks if your brainstorming is going nowhere. Record not what you do each day but your responses and thoughts about each day's experiences. This can be a valuable source of insights and ideas about yourself. Or collect "important moment" articles and interviews from magazines and newspapers. Sports figures and celebrities often recount small but enlightening incidents in their lives in response to interviewers' questions. Or use the résumé you created for your guidance counselor and recommending teachers. You can make an activities list or résumé now if you haven't done so already. Add it all to your brainstorm sheet.

Ask yourself questions: "What are my strengths? My weaknesses?" Do a little soul-searching and be as complete as possible. Add evaluative statements like "I am a stubborn person" or "I like a challenge." Be totally honest.

Now research your topic a little. There aren't any Cliff Notes and there's nothing in the public library. But you can look over your journal, or an old scrapbook or photo album and talk to your parents, friends, employer. Gather ideas about yourself wherever you can. Ask yourself why you do the things you do—what drives you out the front door at 6 a.m. to run five miles, what keeps you up past midnight trying to build a computer program. Ask yourself: What is special about me? What kind of person am I? Under what circumstances do I learn? What interests me? What do I care about? Why is swimming, to me, more a religion than a sport? What is it like growing up in Jerome, Idaho . . . or Needham, Massachusetts . . . or Glendale, Missouri?

Try to create as complete a brainstorm as possible. Do not do this in fifteen minutes one Sunday afternoon. Begin well in advance of the drafting stage and really percolate your topic. A special fringe benefit of taking the college essay seriously is that it can be a learning experience, not just for the college, but for you, too.

Step 2: Focus

Making connections is the next step. You need to analyze your topic and divide it into some manageable pieces. As you saw in the John Hughes brainstorm in Chapter 3, grouping similar ideas and events together highlights patterns in a miscellaneous collection of information. For example, is there a series of volunteer projects? Does your love of math show up in your performance in the state math competition and in your summer job at the computer store? Ask yourself more questions to establish connections, clusters, and groups.

Now focus on three or four important strengths. Keep the unusual, the individual, the vivid. Be positive ("stubborn" isn't a great quality but "committed" is), and don't be afraid of the truth; being honest is the only way to get a fresh and sincere result.

Step 3: Prove

Remember, this is an essay. Your purpose is to persuade the readers of a particular view or interpretation of your subject. That applies as much to a paper on "Dover Beach" as to a paper on you. The first requires specific evidence from the poem. The college essay requires evidence from your life.

Organize your information into a self-outline. List personality characteristics, and under each list five or six pieces of evidence from your life, things you've been or done, that validate your point. Each characteristic is a potential focus for your essay and you need to see which ones are important, which ones you can say something about.

The evidence is crucial. If you've said you're concerned with the welfare of others but can't think of more than one proof, omit it. You're not really motivated by concern for others. You thought you *ought* to be, you thought the college would like to hear that you are. But this is an example of the "institutional response." Forget it!

Look for a potentially interesting and rich focus. As you might toy with opinions about a novel's characters, setting, or foreshadowing techniques, experiment with ideas about your own goals, interests, style. Then see what things have happened to you and what things you have done that support or illuminate these preliminary thesis statements.

Your self-outline might include items like:

1. I like to work with kids
   a. Community House
   b. my little brother
   c. babysitter and mother's helper
   d. Christmas pageant for the church
   e. career interest in child psychology

2. I like classes with student participation
   a. Mr. Stiver's class
   b. drama workshop
   c. Ms. Selman's class

3. I hate sports
   a. gym is dumb
   b. in fourth grade I never got picked for a team
   c. the field hockey jocks are weird (stupid head-bands, weird socks)
   d. I've got enough competition in my life already
   e. I'm uncoordinated (falling off the parallel bars in seventh grade in front of Andrea Kaufman)

4. I always put things off until right before the deadline
   a. this essay
   b. my tenth-grade research paper
   c. getting my yearbook quote done
   d. prom table

Time for more questions. About what have you written the most? What looks interesting, different (but not unflattering)? Are there any career goals here? Motivations for college? Special personal characteristics or experiences? Working with kids might be interesting if your career and college choice are related. The preference for classes with student participation might make a good essay in applying to a college with a special tutorial program. Certainly a loathing for sports is an interesting point. But where can you go with it? Can you use it to show something positive about yourself (maybe your individuality?), something other than just eccentricity or negativity? The procrastination habit is probably not something you want to share with the college; it should be overcome, not glorified.

Again, remember there are no right answers for these questions any more than for any other essay. Admissions committees are diverse groups of individuals; there isn't one thing they want to hear. After reading 20 to 50 essays a day about the charms of University X, the evils of terrorism, and the personal commitment involved in being a doctor, most admissions staffers don't want more essays on "safe" topics. How things are in Paramus, New Jersey, or New Hope, Alabama, might be more engaging. Elizabeth DeLaHunt, an independent counselor in Chicago, laments the self-involved and self-indulgent responses that college essay questions often elicit. "Schools would rather have a sense of the student's place in the world, a sense of his or her relationship—context—as a person."

Looking for the "right" answers is therefore pointless. And it is also counterproductive. The college essay is not an assignment to create a self. "We don't want the back lot at MGM, a created scene over a barren field. We want to see the real landscape," says Bates' Bill Hiss.

When the time comes to write, don't try to find the "right answers." And don't stare at the blank paper and despair. Stare at your self-outline. This prewriting is a good launching pad. By writing about yourself in this format, you will have a beginning and "begun is half done." Don't cheat on this step. Give it plenty of time and attention. Write to write. It will pay off when the drafting begins.

Drafting: Converting the Self-Outline into an Essay

Now consider your questions. With a self-outline, you can plan and create any of the three types of essays required. Several strategies are given for each question. Take your choice. Again, there is no one right answer, no one right essay. Just remember: FOCUS AND PROVE!

Question 1: "Tell Us About Yourself"

Strategy 1: A Standard Essay
With Several Well-Proven Points

The most conservative essay about yourself would be based on two or three of the points from your self-outline and would follow a standard introduction/body/conclusion plan. Look back at Essay 1. The writer attempted one paragraph on family, one on activities, and one on jobs. It is, in fact, a well-organized essay. There is an introduction that identifies the points to be discussed, one point for each body paragraph, and a conclusion that relates the writer to the college. But although the organization of the essay is very good, its weakness is a lack of specifics.

If you choose to write this type of essay, select two or three points from your self-outline, give a paragraph to each, and be sure you give *plenty* of evidence. Don't try to do too much: two or at most three points should do it. Either choose things not apparent from the rest of your application or "light up" some of the activities and experiences listed there. Make it vivid. The difference between general (and forgettable) and specific (and interesting) can be seen in the following first and final drafts of one paragraph from a student's essay.

Example 1

The job I had this past summer expanded my level of maturity and provided me with exposure to a world which I had not previously experienced. It involved a combination of a job as doorman and a custodial worker in a New York apartment building. This job allowed me to break out of my shell and see the spectrum of the world as a whole. I have learned balance and adaptability. And I can empathize with the hard-working people of the so-called lower class for many of them are now my friends.

Example 2

The job I had this past summer introduced me to physical labor and some new attitudes. I worked a forty-hour week as a doorman and custodian at the Renoir, an apartment building with 120 units on East 78th Street in Manhattan. I had a black tuxedo with a striped vest for half my day and, for the rest of the day, a paint-spattered blue and white jumpsuit that said 'Howie' on the pocket. In either outfit, I often found I was ignored by the people I helped. I got a little more acknowledgment in the tuxedo. I never got a 'Hello' but I did get a few 'Thank you's' from the people I held the door for. As the custodian, I was invisible. I could go four or five hours without hearing a single word directly addressed to me. From this job, I think I learned something about New York, about furnaces, and about the human temperament when deprived of air conditioning. But I also learned something about how our society treats people who do manual labor.

There's nothing wrong with a standard essay about yourself; just give plenty of time to building up and making specific the paragraph development that proves each of your points. Do not substitute a list of activities for support. Make a point about yourself in each paragraph and then present evidence to illuminate it, to back it up.

Strategy 2: Less Is More

For many years, Yale suggested applicants write an essay about interests, activities, background, or aspirations; they got a lot of four-paragraph essays, with one paragraph for interests, one for activities, one for background, and one for aspirations. They changed their question to avoid this "laundry list" kind of response.

You might want to draft a standard essay (Strategy 1) and then mine it for the most interesting and important point about yourself. This is especially useful if your essay is supposed to be one paragraph or half a page. Essay 1, at the beginning of this chapter, distilled to its best and most vivid paragraph, could be very effective. The writer wanted to explain the importance of her family, but she tried to do it in only two sentences! She might have done better with an essay on just that one idea—her family's support. She could have used her page to *show* the half inch of rain that fell on her first varsity field hockey game (and on her mother and father). To this picture of soggy family devotion she might have tied her extracurricular involvement and the source of her own commitment to help others. There's a lot to be said for taking a small focus and really *showing* it to the reader.

The student who wrote about his summer job also ended up using a "less is more" strategy. He had originally begun with an essay of several paragraphs—one for clubs, one for sports, one for jobs (Example 1), and one for career plans. The final essay focused only on the summer job and tied it to several other revealing points. Drafting helped him identify the best point; other ideas were subordinated to it. He ended up with two strong paragraphs (one given in Example 2) instead of four flabby ones. (See Sample 1 in Chapter 6 for a personal essay that focuses on five minutes of dipping ice cream.)

Cleopatra had herself delivered to Antony rolled up in an Oriental carpet. I imagine it was a rather memorable delivery. The "less is more" essay makes a vivid self-presentation from within a simple (even ordinary) framework.

Strategy 3: The Narrative Essay

The most focused and narrow approach to the "Tell us about yourself" question is a short and vivid story. Omit the introduction, write one or two narrative paragraphs that grab and engage the reader's attention, then show how this little tale reveals you. Sample 3 in Chapter 6 uses something like this strategy. The writer begins with an introduction, then tells the story of a conversation from which he draws a picture of himself, his background, his insights. This type of essay puts the proof first and the focus last. See Sample 7 in Chapter 6. It's a little more risky but it can be very interesting. If you're a good writer, give it a try; if not, rely on a more conservative strategy.

Your procedure for the "You" question is:

1. Brainstorm yourself toward a self-outline.
2. Focus on several of your distinctive qualities.
3. Prove what you say with extensive and vivid evidence.
4. Use several proofs or a fully described incident for each body paragraph; do not write a list of activities, a travelog, or an autobiography. Avoid pure chronology.
5. Choose one of the following:
   - a standard essay with several equal focus points in several well-developed body paragraphs
   - a "less-is-more" essay that uses one experience to make several points
   - a short narrative that leads to your focus

6. *Be specific!* None of these styles of a "tell-us-about-yourself" essay will hurt you as long as you remember to make it concrete, detailed, vivid.

Question 2: "Why Did You Select College X?"

The focus and the proof for "Why Us?" questions are provided: The focus is the connection between you and the school; the proof is in the catalog. Review the pluses of the school and how you came to choose it. Find connections between the college and the points on your self-outline. Then decide what percentage of the essay ought to treat the school and what percentage ought to treat you.

Strategy 1: A Standard Essay on the School's Pluses

Using the standard introduction/body/conclusion format, you can write an essay whose body paragraphs are the points about the school that are attractive to you as a prospective freshman. Do some research. Read the course catalog and viewbook carefully, and see what is offered that appeals to you. From this you can focus on the main connection between you and the school. Your body might begin with one paragraph on small points—location, climate, size, the composition of the student body—and build to one or two paragraphs on the more significant factors—curriculum offerings, class settings (tutorials, conferences, mass lectures), majors, special programs.

If you're sure of your career goal, make this your thesis; then show what the school has to offer in your particular area of concentration. Be sure they do have what you need and want. This is as important for you as it is for them. Is the faculty first rate? (Ask friends or teachers about the faculty roster.) Are there some well-known people in your field teaching there? Does the library have a unique section devoted to American political science, Judaica, the letters of Ernest Hemingway? Do some research and mention specific factors that tie in with your primary interest. For example, if you plan to concentrate in international relations, you might mention the college's Chinese language and literature program, its Junior Year Abroad option, or the short-term work-study program at the United Nations.

Avoid an ingratiating tone. Instead, *prove* whatever you say. Point out the real advantages of a particular school or program.

> I've always wanted to work in the health care field. But how I want to do this is still not clear to me. That's why Georgetown's nursing school appeals to me. I want at least a B.S., rather than just an R.N. I don't want to feel "different" from the rest of the undergraduate body, and I like the idea of mixed undergraduate housing. The nursing/pre-medical option also seems right for me since I am still considering medical school.

It's to your advantage as a potential freshman to scrutinize the place where you will live for four years, become an adult, and spend in excess of $100,000. Your answer, paragraph or essay, should show your interest and prove the school's distinctiveness in that area. It will become apparent if a school was chosen whimsically or because your boyfriend is a junior there. Dig in, find out, and then use your knowledge.

Strategy 2: The School and You

Some colleges ask for an essay that connects you to them:

"Assess your reasons for wanting to attend college. How have your previous experiences influenced your current academic and/or career plans?"

This is an essay primarily about you. It asks only secondarily about your choice of college. Write a personal essay as suggested in Strategy 1 or 2 of the "Tell Us About Yourself" question. Then use the conclusion to make a connection to the college. The second type of conclusion discussed in Chapter 3, one that serves as a springboard for futher ideas, may be helpful here.

In Essay 1 on page 85 the writer set out to show the importance of her college choice in her conclusion, but there was no substance to her paragraph. Had she mentioned the college's preprofessional studies in law or its special 3-2 program in nursing she would have created a real connection between her plans to help others and her choice of college. Wherever you show why College X is for you, be specific and well informed.

Your procedure for the "Why Us" question is:

1. Brainstorm yourself toward a self-outline.
2. Research the college for the qualities that make it special to you.
3. Connect yourself to the college. Select one of the following:
   - Make several body paragraphs from these connections, building toward the most important ones.
   - Write an essay about yourself that comes to the *conclusion* that X is the college for you.
4. Research is the key to good proof; highlight *real* connections between you and the college.
5. Avoid an ingratiating tone. BE SPECIFIC.

Question 3: Be Creative

Strategy 1: Begin With You and Let That Dictate a Choice

If you have a creative question, there is again some built-in help. If you've been directed to write about a lunchmate, book, or photo, consult your self-outline and with a suitable focus select the topic that corresponds to a particular quality of yours.

If you're artistic, have lunch with Georgia O'Keefe and make your conversation with her reveal your interests in art. If you're a violin virtuoso, nominate Isaac Stern for man of the year and *show* that you know why he deserves it. You're a creative soul? Send Vassar a photo of your Grateful Dead Halloween costume. In an essay about the creation of the outfit and other similar activities, *show* them you have the imagination and skills to conceive and execute other original ideas. Harvard liked an application essay about chocolate; the writer used her job in a candy store to show her insight, judgment, and creativity.

You can use a standard essay form here. The focus is your choice. Your body paragraphs should describe the pleasures of that book, the advantages of lunch with Charles Darwin, or the three major changes you would enact at your high school. Again, remember that it is the specifics that will make or break this essay. Sample 4 in Chapter 6 fails not because the author wanted to have lunch with Monet, but because she did not know enough about him. Read up a little on your dinner guest, review that novel you've chosen, talk to your high school principal. Your initiative and sincerity will show in the specificity of your end result.

Strategy 2: A Production Piece

Shakespeare said, "the poet's pen/ Turns [things unknown] to shapes, and gives to airy nothing/ A local habitation and a name." An essay may, likewise, in a variety of ways, give a "local habitation and a name" to you. A purely creative essay can reveal your imagination, willingness to take a risk, creativity, and insight. If the question is totally without limits, an imaginative piece may demonstrate the most about you.

Audrey Smith, director of admission at Hampshire, says, "We hope to get a sense of the person, the individual. The vehicle can be almost anything." Thus, it is almost impossible to give advice. It is helpful only to say that some students have found that a sense of themselves as individuals was most evident in an original piece—a meditation on their nickname, a speculation about elm trees, a hypothesis about socks (see Sample 5 in Chapter 6). It's risky, but for some students, it is the right risk and very effective. You're on your own with this one; good luck!

The procedure for the creative question is:

1. Brainstorm yourself toward a self-outline.
2. Choose a representative quality from the self-outline.

3. Connect this quality to a choice that will illuminate it: an artist if painting is important to you, the charms of Faulkner if you're a budding writer, and so on. Be sincere and do not try to choose "what you think they want."
4. Research your choice.
5. Write a SPECIFIC and vivid defense of your subject.
6. Get a second opinion.

Summary

A standard essay, well-organized and specific in its focus and proof, is a reasonable answer for any question. Neither predictable answers nor innovative choices make memorable essays unless you SHOW the rightness of the choice. Bill Clinton is a better choice than Bruce Springsteen for man of the year only if you argue it persuasively. A very good case could be made for Springsteen, too, but only if you've got four great reasons and lots of evidence from specific events and music to back it up. FOCUS AND PROVE, no matter what!

The dangers are not in the topics themselves. When admissions people complain about travelogs and autobiographies, it is the lack of focus, the broad angle that is the downfall of these essays. When counselors advise students against responses about trips, sports, twins, divorces, it's because lack of proof, the generality of these essays, can be a problem. Memorable essays on any of these topics exist, by writers who took a narrow focus and backed it up with plenty of vivid specifics. Choose a strategy that feels comfortable, and be specific.

The High Risk Essay

Does the following dilemma sound familiar to you? "I'm about to apply to a school with 13,000 applicants and 1,300 places. Is it wise to aim for a big impact? I need a high-powered performance that's going to get me in!"

Keep in mind that, although the essay is important, no single aspect of the application can get you into a college. The essay can make a difference but it is not sensible to believe that a knock-out essay will get you into a school you're not generally qualified to attend. Don't try to do something that will "make up for all the rest" of your application—it will only lead to embarrassment and disappointment.

Okay, you are a qualified applicant for this school, but you need to stand out. You've decided you want to be different. You've had it with "safe" and decided you want to write an essay that is a "powerful tipper" for your case. Can it be done? Maybe.

Think of the Academy Awards. Well over a hundred people make similar acceptance speeches that night. What makes any of them stand out in our memories?

1. *Surprise* does. Some acceptance speeches say things we aren't expecting to hear. You could write about a point from your self-outline that few other writers would choose. For example, instead of writing about your concern for children, you could write about why you hate sports.

2. *Form* can do it. Some speakers surprise us not with what they say but with how they say it. A narrative essay may have enough suspense (if it isn't too long) to give this added element. The essay on a job in a candy store included a chocolate Veritas (Harvard's motto). It won't get an applicant accepted, but it is memorable.

3. The *unusual* can grab lagging attention. Special circumstances—and I mean really special—can make a distinctive essay. "When I first realized that my mother was deaf, it did not affect me much at all; my transactions between the deaf world and the hearing world had become a matter of course. . . ."

   Supplementary materials may help here, too. The student who described a 250-toothpick bridge that supported 286 pounds and won him a physics competition made it real by sending the bridge along. But think a long time about sending support material. Send only something individual, of very high quality, and related to the total impact of your application. The toothpick bridge would not have enhanced the application if seven others were sent, if it had supported only eight pounds, or if the applicant were a music major. Research the admissions committee a little before you send anything. If faculty are involved, tapes, artwork, and projects may get more attention. But remember the volume of applications that have to be reviewed and don't expect more than your share of attention.

4. *Humor* usually works—*real* humor. A lot of high school humor is goofy, embarrassing, or in poor taste. Just remember Noel Coward's advice: "Wit ought to be a glorious treat, like caviar. Never spread it about like marmalade." Get a second (and a third) opinion.

5. And, of course, *shock* can do the job . . . either for or against you. You want to be clever not silly, a risk taker not a fool. John Bunnell, associate dean and director of admission at Stanford, cautions that, "The problem is there's a thin line between being humorous and being flip, between being creative and being eccentric. Taking risks is not a negative quality but there ought to be some common sense involved." Applicants who, given one day in time to spend with anyone in history, choose Cindy Crawford haven't thought much about their options.

You have to weigh the risk. Of course, there is often a high reward where there is a high risk. It takes something special to get a reader to say, "Hey, Alice, listen to this one!" And I am sure in the final hours of committee meetings on "gray zone" applications, no one has ever said, "Hey, wait a minute, what about that kid who wrote the essay about his *family?*"

But the predictable essay doesn't damn its author as much as a tasteless and vulgar attempt to astonish and surprise. Write about whatever makes you comfortable. Take a chance if that's your nature. You may find a like-minded individual on the committee who champions your application because of your essay. Whatever you write should be specific. And do get a couple of opinions on it; long hours at a desk can blur your sense of right versus ridiculous.

Editing ▬▬▬▬▬▬▬▬▬▬▬▬▬▬

A Word About Word Processing

Computers are here to stay. First graders are hacking away at Mac's and most high schools offer a variety of courses in computing, computer languages, and applications. Some colleges, like Drew University and Stevens Institute of Technology, issue students their own computers when they enroll. Other schools have writing centers where students can use microcomputers for their writing assignments. Your high school may have such a facility.

If you have followed the time line suggested in Chapter 1 and are not working against an immediate deadline, begin your college essay on a computer. Brainstorming may be a lot easier with a keyboard and screen than with pencil and paper, and any assignment benefits from the revision and editing capabilities of a computer.

You will draft, redraft, and edit the college essay many times, and you may want to recycle and revise it into several versions for different colleges. The computer allows you to make modifications quickly and painlessly and then, while saving the original version of your paper, it will print a neat copy of the latest version without adding any new errors. You are more likely to write eight different essays truly tailored to each school if it's almost as easy to do as making eight copies of one essay. (And wouldn't it be nice to have a built-in spelling checker to hunt down and identify your errors?)

It is not worthwhile, however, to purchase a personal computer for one use; you may want to investigate whether some of the following places offer computer time:

- The high school writing center (or computer classroom after school)
- A relative's office
- The local college writing center (they might let you rent some time)
- A computer center that charges by the hour for use of their equipment

A few words of caution. Proofread carefully. Neatly typed pages tend to look perfect when they often are not. Read drafts several times. Sometimes the thorny problem areas signaled in handwritten drafts by multiple cross-outs and arrows fail to stand out on typed pages. Read the copy on the screen and then in a final hard copy draft before the last printout. The typographical errors of a computer often are different from the traditional errors of a typewriter; reformatting problems, incomplete deletions, and misplaced insertions are the new kinds of errors to look for.

Don't be overconfident just because you're using a fancy, expensive machine. Alas, it only does what you tell it to do. Revising your Bryn Mawr essay for Dartmouth is a poor idea if you forget to delete references to the advantages of living in the Philadelphia area. No matter how you produce your essay, proofread it carefully several times. See Sample 8 in Chapter 6.

Handwritten essays are harder to read, so do type if possible. If the application specifically asks, as some do, for your own handwriting, make sure it's legible and not crammed onto the page. I once had a student who had "dumb" handwriting. Lisa was very bright but she had big, loopy handwriting and she dotted her "i's" with cute little circles. I tried to explain to her that most people would pick up a paper like hers with a preconception that it was going to be a "C" performance at best. We finally agreed that typing her papers would free her from this subtle liability. Keep this in mind if you decide that typing takes too much time. You can always print your essays and attach them to the application.

Editing Tips

No matter how you draft and write your essay, you will want to edit it. Remember your goal: to introduce yourself to the admissions committee. And remember your strategy: focus and prove. Reread your essay once to be sure you have zeroed in on one or two illuminating ideas about yourself and have *shown* them to your reader with plenty of specifics.

Then read the essay a second time. Look for spelling errors, sentence fragments, and confused expressions. Rewrite and revise. Some sentences cannot be improved and must be cut. When in doubt, strike it out.

Read the essay again for style.

1. Remember that good writing has a natural, easy-to-read quality. Keep the language and structure simple, direct, and clear. Don't try to hide shoddy thinking behind elaborate language. Use the fewest and simplest words possible.
2. Strike a balance between a personal and a formal tone. In a choice between a long, fancy word and a short, simple one, choose the simple word:
   a. The reason for this predicament is that the local hardware store does not have the extensive financial resources needed in order to be able to stock every size of every hardware item.

b. Hardware stores can't afford much variety.

a. Having been involved in theater arts activities for many years, on a wide variety of levels ranging from high school to independent repertory theater, I have naturally gained a fairly comprehensive acting experience.
b. My knowledge of acting comes from high school productions and independent repertory theater work.

a. I have an intense affinity for learning in a liberal arts environment that has extensive course offerings from which to choose.
b. I want the choices that a liberal arts education offers.

The language used in the "a" samples distances the reader, something you do not want to do in your college essay. Avoid the thesaurus, be yourself, and don't substitute a stuffy style for substance.

3. Remember that your audience is the admissions committee, not the English faculty's poet-in-residence or the chairman of the chemistry department. They are reading hundreds of applications. They are a group of individuals with individual ideas of what the college needs and wants. They are not scholars, and they are pressed for time. Be intelligent and knowledgeable, but above all, be yourself. See Sample 10 in Chapter 6.

4. Avoid clichés and sentences that sound good but don't mean anything. For example, don't end with a line like, "I'll bring as much to College X as X will give to me." "To learn, to love, to live" sounds great—alliteration always sounds great—but it doesn't say much. Make every sentence count.

5. Avoid worn-out literary sources. Forget "to thine own self be true." Over-used quotations, old saws, and familiar maxims will sap the freshness of your performance.

6. Don't "sling the bull." Using words carelessly or inaccurately will only hurt your chances.

7. Use active verbs and vigorous expression. Instead of "Due to my parents' coaxing, I decided to try once more" say "My parents

coaxed me to try again." Instead of "My interest in sports was encouraged by my father" say "My father encouraged my football career."

8. Avoid empty words and phrases like "really," "special," "unique," "interesting," "each and every," and "meaningful."

9. Avoid vague and predictable conclusions: "I learned a lot," "I interacted with others different from myself," "I benefited from the love and support of my family," "I learned to work with others."

10. Proofread, proofread, proofread. The essay that began, "If there is one word that can describe me, that word is 'profectionist,'" did not make a favorable impression on the admissions committee at Bates. An admission staffer who graduated the previous June or a senior student intern may not disqualify you for grammatical errors, but why take the chance? Essays are read as an indication of writing skill. You might get the chairman of the English department as your reader! See Sample 11 in Chapter 6.

Now put it all away for a week. Then reread it two more times for errors. Your essay doesn't have to win a Pulitzer prize but it should show both effort and commitment in its clarity, specificity, and correctness.

Making the Essay Yours

Colleges expect you to get some help with your essay. Your counselor might talk to you about choosing a subject and your parents or a teacher might help proofread a final draft. These are legitimate steps of the brainstorming and editing processes and all writers get some of this kind of help.

But only you can write your essay. The essay should introduce you to the college and no one else can speak for you but yourself.

Just as you would not use someone else's SAT scores or falsify your grades, you must not include any part of a published work or another student's writing in your college essay. This is plagiarism and, if it is discovered, your application will be denied. Your high school will be informed and all of your applications may be affected. Even if you're not caught, you have misrepresented yourself to the school. You don't want to end up at a college knowing that you got in on false presences.

Don't let someone else write your essay for you either. Do not use a service that offers to help you with your essay "line by line, if needed," for a fee. Colleges are not the enemy anxious to find a reason to deny you admission. As a general rule, the right credentials for the right school will not be ignored. Many schools in this country accept the majority of their applicants. You and the school are in a cooperative process of "mating." Misrepresenting yourself cannot help; it's neither satisfying nor mature. If you are ready to go to college, then you are ready to accept your successes and failures as your own. Do it yourself!

Summary

No matter what questions you have to answer, begin with yourself. Brainstorm and focus on one or two points that will introduce and illuminate you to the admissions committee.

Then select your strategy. Write a short, legible, and correct essay, standard or varietal, that SHOWS the qualities about you that you have chosen to illuminate with vivid specifics, not generalities.

Revise, proofread, and type it up. Photocopy your various application packets and mail them off. Check with your recommending teachers and with the guidance office to be sure they've contributed their share. Then relax. If you've followed the time line and the steps outlined in this book, once the colleges to which you've applied have made their decisions, you will probably have the luxury of yet another opportunity to choose.

Analyzing Eleven Essays

The eleven sample essays that follow demonstrate a variety of strengths and weaknesses. None is presented as a perfect or "correct" college essay. Marlyn Lewis, director of admission at Harvard, says the essay is "a very important part of the application, and in some ways the most personal part." Thus for admissions personnel, "there is no one standard." These samples are meant to suggest the number of options you have in introducing yourself to a college.

Sample 1

I've been told by many of my friends, teachers, and relatives that majoring in English is stupid. Whenever I tell people what I intend to do, they look at me as if I've said that I intend to major in Frisbee or creative gum chewing. These doubting Thomases invariably inform me that English majors all over the country are eating in soup kitchens and collecting welfare checks. They tell me that a liberal arts education is nothing more than a four-year escape from life, and that I should put my intelligence to some better use such as business education or chemistry. Nature, however, never geared me for these fields. Obviously, my genes have predestined me for fiscal failure.

I do, of course, have a practical side that warns me, "Susan, that's all well and good but how can you expect to get anywhere with a major in English? Let's face it, kid, the people who are warning you away from English know from experience that being a wordmonger is, at best, a risky business. "

If I were like many people, my solid practical side would win out. I would dutifully throw away my complete Shakespeare and shop around for a quickie Berlitz course in COBOL. I would probably get richer quicker if I took practical courses in college and forgot about English. But I just can't compromise my belief that learning to use the English language is a timely and sensible thing to do.

My cousin, who recently graduated from Wesleyan University with a major in art, is now trying to find work as a waiter. My grandfather sees this as a prime indicator that I should go into investment banking. I, however, fail to see anything devastating about waiting on tables. In fact, one of the nicest things I ever experienced occurred when I was working at Dairy Delight.

My job as a salesperson and ice cream scooper is not particularly lucrative or challenging, but it keeps me in records and clothes. It also serves as a great opportunity to meet people. One night I was behind the counter when two men came to the window. As I poised my pencil to take their order, I was confronted with a request unlike any I had ever heard. The confused-looking man said, "My wife wants something like a dipped, almond walnut maple butter krinkle koated sugar cone. Maybe I'd better go back and ask her what she meant."

I, however, sensing a challenge, said, "Wait, I bet I know what she wants. Could it be that she wants a double scoop of butter almond and maple walnut ice cream in krinkle koat on a sugar cone?" The man breathed a sigh of relief and agreed I was probably right.

As I portioned out the ice cream, I couldn't help but think how funny the man's request had sounded. When I handed him the cone, I drawled, "Here's your super dooper double scoop of krinkle koated flipped out skipped out joy food."

The man just grinned and said, "Oh, that's what those things are called!" Then he ordered a hot tin roof, hold the butterscotch. I returned with a "comble chaud, sans la bourre d'Ecosse." My customers were suitably impressed. The second man ordered a coffee ice cream cone, and my muse rolled over and died. Returning with his order, I sighed, "Here's your cone. I'm creatively spent!"

In all, the order took about five minutes to fill, and between the antics I can remember and sundry other ridiculous things I can't, I was almost disgustingly entertaining. When the order was finally filled, and I tried to hand the men their change, they said, "Oh, please keep it. And thank you so much!" As they left, I just grinned and went back to work, but that fifty-two cents meant a lot to me. It meant that somebody really enjoyed the games I was playing with words, and that even the most mundane job can be fun if it's approached in the right way. During that night, I sang the theme song from Casablanca with a baseball coach who thinks he's Bogie, discussed Marxism with a little old lady, and heard more than I ever wanted to know about some woman's gall bladder operation.

I have aspirations of accomplishing something far more meaningful than scooping ice cream. But if going to college for four years helps me to appreciate and manipulate the English language, then at the very least it can help me to become one of the happiest ice cream scoopers in the world.

Things To Notice About This Essay

1. It has a clear and continual *focus:* using the English language.
2. It has *proof* of her interest in language: the story of the two men and the ice cream. She is specific not only in this story, but also throughout the essay (her determination to pursue English despite others' opinions, her complete set of Shakespeare, COBOL, the gall bladder).
3. It begins with a great first line and uses the "common misperception" introduction (even though it took her three paragraphs to get going). She details the idea that language study is a waste of time and then ends paragraph three with her thesis: "learning to use the English language is a timely and sensible thing to do."
4. Her tone is personal and her style is fairly casual. The essay gives us a sense of the person, a look at her interests, values, style, and humor that her numbers and scores can't show.
5. The body of the essay is primarily narrative, but it is with a small incident, not a life history, that she proves her interest in language.
6. Her conclusion is a standard summary that connects her aspirations to her college decision. It also relates to the rest of her application, a recommendation made by an English teacher, and scores on the verbal section of the SAT.

Sample 2 ━━━━━━━━━━━━━━

From the time I was able to realize what a university was, all I heard from my mother's side of the family was about the University of Michigan and the great heritage it has. Many a Saturday afternoon my grandfather would devote to me, by sitting me down in front of the television and reminiscing about the University of Michigan while halftime occurred during a Michigan Wolverines football game. Later, as I grew older and universities took on greater meaning, my mother and uncle, both alumni of the University of Michigan, took me to see their old stamping grounds. From first sight, the university looked frightening because of its size, but with such a large school comes diversity of people and of academic and non-academic events.

In Springfield High School, non-academic clubs such as the Future Physicians and the Pylon, both of which I have belonged to for two years, give me an opportunity to see both the business world and the medical world. These two clubs have given me a greater sense of what these careers may be like. In Future Physicians, I participated in field trips to children's hospitals and also participated in two bloodbanks.

Currently I hold a job at Maas Brothers. This lets me interact with people outside my own immediate environment. I meet different kinds of people, in different moods, with different attitudes, and with different values. This job teaches me to be patient with people, to have responsibility, and to appreciate people for what they are.

In the community I am active in my church Youth Group. As a high school sophomore, I was our church's representative to the Diocesan Youth Fellowship. I helped organize youth group events, the largest being "The Bishop's Ball," a state-wide event for 300 young people. I also played high school junior varsity soccer for two years. As a senior I will be playing varsity soccer, but in the off-season. As a junior I coached a girls' soccer team for the town. This gave me a great deal of responsibility, because the care of twenty-four girls was put into my custody. It felt very satisfying to pass on the knowledge of soccer to another generation. The girls played teams from other parts of Florida. Though their record was 3-8, the girls enjoyed their season. This is what I taught them was the greatest joy of soccer.

The past three years of my life have given me greater visions of my future. I see the University of Michigan as holding a large book with many unread chapters and myself as an eager child who has just learned to read. I intend to read and probe into all the chapters. The University of Michigan offers me more than the great reputation of this fine school, but a large student body with diverse likes and dislikes, and many activities, both academic and non-academic, to participate in. With the help of the University of Michigan, I will be successful after college and be able to make a name and place for myself in our society.

Things To Notice About This Essay ━━━━━

1. It follows a general essay organization, with an introduction, several body paragraphs about different activities, and a conclusion that returns to the earlier idea of Michigan's diversity.
2. It has no focus but rather jumps around from the school to the writer and from point to point. Notice especially the lack of transition from the first paragraph to the second: how did we get from Michigan's diversity to the writer's clubs?

3. The body paragraphs lack *proof:* what are these clubs and jobs, what did he do in each one, how many field trips were taken, and what was his role?

4. What's Pylon? What does he do at Maas Brothers?

5. There are plenty of generalizations but no evidence to back up any of them. How did these activities give him a greater sense of the career world? "Participated" and "interact" are pretty vague words. Compare the discussion of Maas Brothers with the ice cream scooper's story.

6. There is very little specific knowledge of what the University of Michigan has to offer.

7. The style is rather stuffy and awkward ("while halftime occurred," "the care of twenty-four girls was put into my custody").

8. Most important, nearly everything described here appears elsewhere on the application, under sports, jobs, extracurricular activities, and alumni connections.

9. The writer would be well advised to focus on *one* of the things discussed in this essay. Perhaps he could show the reader his work with the girls' soccer team. What he did to make Jennifer and Gretchen and Courtney enjoy soccer even though they only won three of their games would be more focused and vivid than a lot of talk about passing things on to future generations.

10. In short, the essay seems full of information and displays adequate form, but it lacks *focus* and *proof.*

Sample 3

My most important experience sought me out. It happened to me; I didn't cause it.

My preferred companions are books or music or pen and paper. I have only a small circle of close friends, few of whom get along together. They could easily be counted "misfits." To be plain, I found it quite easy to doubt my ability to have any sort of "close relationship."

After the closing festivities of Andover Summer School this past summer, on the night before we were scheduled to leave, a girl I had met during the program's course approached me. She came to my room and sat down on my bed and announced that she was debating with herself whether she wanted me to become her boyfriend. She wanted my reaction, my opinion.

I was startled, to say the least, and frightened. I instantly said, "No." I told her I on no account wanted this and that I would reject any gestures she made towards starting a relationship. I would ignore her entirely, if need be. I explained that I was a coward. I wanted nothing whatsoever to do with a relationship. I talked a lot and very fast.

To my surprise, she did not leave instantly. Instead, she hugged her knees and rocked back and forth on my bed. I watched her from across the room. She rocked, and I watched. Doubts crept up on me. Opportunity had knocked and the door was still locked. It might soon depart.

"I lied," I said. "I was afraid of what might happen if we became involved. But it's better to take the chance than to be afraid."

She told me she knew I had lied. I had made her realize, though, how much she actually wanted me to be her boyfriend. We decided to keep up a relationship after Andover.

Even then, I was not sure which had been the lie. Now I think that everything I said may have been true when I said it. But I'm still not sure.

I learned, that night, that I could be close to someone. I also realize, now, that it doesn't matter whether or not that person is a misfit; the only important thing is the feeling, the closeness, the connection. As long as there is something between

two people—friendship, love, shared interests, whatever else—
it is a sign that there can be some reconciliation with fear,
some "fit" for misfits. And it shows that fear need not always
win, that we can grow and change, and even have second
chances.

I am still seeing her.

Things To Notice About This Essay

1. It follows the standard essay pattern: an introduction (short), a series of supporting paragraphs for the body, a conclusion (here, two paragraphs, a summary paragraph and an end sentence).
2. It has a *focus:* his anxiety about relationships.
3. It has *proof:* the story of his conversation with a girl. Again, focused narrative development has made the proof vivid.
4. It is short, to the point, simple, and yet memorable. It is interesting without being grand, noble, or cosmic.
5. The style is simple and direct, employing short sentences and simple words to tell a simple story.
6. It coordinates and enriches an application full of academic achievements and high scores and grades. It is definitely not something found elsewhere in the application.

Sample 4

Claude Monet, an impressionist painter, challenged the traditional ideas of nineteenth-century art. He was an individual who had the courage to follow his convictions and, as a result, was not accepted by the critics of his time.

Had Monet lived in New York City in the early twentieth century, he might have enjoyed the ambiance of Greenwich Village, a place similar to the Left Bank of Paris. The Village offers young artists a creative environment in which they can meet and exchange ideas. I would invite Monet to share a bottle of Chablis at a nearby sidewalk cafe.

Due to the fact the Salon never accepted Monet's paintings, he never sold any. Monet was not discouraged by their disapproval. He suggested to a few of his contemporaries to set up their own show in opposition to the Salon. This exhibit was not well received by the critics; however, a few people actually responded favorably to these innovative paintings. Shortly thereafter, Monet developed a following that appreciated his art.

One of the questions I would ask Monet was how he found the courage to challenge the established standards mandated by the Salon. He expressed his belief that his artistic expression was acceptable. He was willing to defend his style despite the consequences. Monet's response would help me realize that if you believe in something strongly enough, you must have the faith to defend it.

Claude Monet was a man who was able to stand up for his beliefs and act upon his convictions. I hope if I were ever confronted with a similar situation, I would be able to draw upon the same courage Monet did and stand by my beliefs.

Things To Notice About This Essay ▬▬▬

1. It follows proper essay form, although it takes two paragraphs out of five (too great a percentage) to introduce the idea of lunch with Monet.
2. It has a *focus:* lunch with Monet would be a chance to discuss standing by one's convictions.
3. It lacks *proof:* only brief and vague mention is made of what Monet suffered for his convictions. Two short paragraphs are

meant to do all the work. Little knowledge of Impressionism, Monet's life, or art in France in the 1870s is revealed. For example, Monet sold many paintings during his lifetime; the writer doesn't know her subject well enough. She may have chosen this topic for the impression she hoped it would create rather than because of her interest in Monet.

4. The admissions committee looks for a connection between the essay and the rest of the application. Only a very slim connection is made here to the writer herself; she does not present herself as an art major or as a rebel. Therefore, the essay fails to support the rest of the application.

Sample 5

It has come to my attention that our nation, and nations like ours, have long been plagued by a mysterious occurrence. An occurrence that is as perplexing as it is frustrating, and as baffling as it is widespread, a problem that finds its origins at the very foot of our society. The problem of which I speak is none other than "The Orphan Sock Enigma," the constant disappearance of individual socks during the laundering process. It is a problem familiar to all of us, and also one to which we have unwillingly admitted defeet [sic].

I recently decided that this puzzle had remained unsolved for too long, and resolved to find an explanation. (In the grand tradition of science, I refused to be discouraged by the basic irrelevance of my cause.) But the truth that I uncovered is more shocking and fantastic than I could have ever imagined. My procedures, observations, and conclusions are as follows:

First, to verify that the problem exists, experimental and control loads of laundry were completely processed (put through the washer and dryer). In the experimental load (load with socks), by the end of the process, some socks were lost. But in the control load (load without socks), no socks were lost. Thus, the problem was verified.

Next the progress of a load of socks was carefully monitored. The results indicated that sock disappearance occurs during the period of time when the load is in the dryer. Following this conclusion, a literature search was done and a very significant fact was uncovered: there is no mention of socks disappearing in dryers before the invention of dryers in the 1920s. All evidence clearly pointed to the dryer. And it is there that I would find the answer to the enigma.

Then, the actual experiment was done. In four separate trials, a number of socks (ten socks, or five pairs) were put through a normal drying cycle. The types of socks tested were selected by the highly accurate Harvey-Allman Principle Hierarchy and Zero Alternative Reduction Dimension (HAP-HAZARD).

The mass of the total load was measured prior to processing. Upon completion of the cycle, the mass of the remaining load plus the lint collected was also measured. In addition, the temperature of a running, empty dryer was measured, as was the temperature of a running, full dryer during the cycle. A table of data follows.

In each and every trial, one or two of the socks were lost (each from a different pair). More importantly, in each and every trial, there was a net loss of mass and also a net increase in temperature. These results suggested a test hypothesis. Through the use of Einstein's equation for mass-energy equivalence, $E = mc^2$, the net loss of mass was completely and totally accounted for by the net increase in temperature. All the evidence clearly pointed to one unavoidable, momentous conclusion: all the socks that had been

TRIAL #	#1	#2	#3	#4
Initial Mass 10 socks	265g	270g	276g	261g
Final Mass remaining socks and lint	261g	266g	271g	256g
Temp. running, empty dryer	65.56°C	65.56°C	65.56°C	65.56°C
Temp. running, dryer with socks	70.56°C	70.56°C	71.56°C	71.56°C
Net change in mass	4.0g	4.0g	5.0g	5.0g
Net change in temp.	5.0°C	5.0°C	6.25°C	6.25°C

Mass and temperature data for trials 1-4.

disappearing in countries all over the world had been directly converted to energy (or that there was something seriously wrong with my dryer). I have just begun to realize the monumental importance and far-reaching implications of my discovery. Quite possibly, it could completely change the way we live our lives (and do our laundry) for years to come.

From further experimentation, it seems that the amount of energy liberated (and mass lost) is directly related to the amount of the fiber Spandex in the sock.

But for some reason, the Spandex must be in the form of a sock for the reaction to take place. Therefore, by increasing the amount of Spandex in a sock, one can increase the amount of energy liberated. It also seems that the reaction can be controlled by the presence of different numbers of fabric softening sheets, similar to the effect of control rods in a nuclear reactor. In light of these discoveries, my house is now completely powered by a "Sock Reactor."

Fig. 1. Simplified Diagram of a "Sock Reactor."

I estimate that just a few "Sock Reactors" could supply power to a city the size of Chicago with zero danger (provided a good supply of fabric softening sheets is on hand). This is because one hundred percent of the mass is completely converted into energy safely, easily, and without leaving any of that unsightly radioactive waste common to those other name brand reactors. Therefore, you and your loved ones are spared from that embarrassing radiation sickness and unpleasant aftertaste.

Originally, I had hoped to keep knowledge of this discovery fairly restricted, but I fear that word has leaked out. I have reason to believe there is a merger planned between Interwoven Hosiery and General Power nuclear division.

Although I have not been able to explain why only one sock out of a pair can be converted, it appears to in some way relate to a black hole, a time warp, and static cling.

Albert Einstein, the man who first discovered the mass-energy equivalence, never wore socks. I think that just about says it all.

Things To Notice About This Essay

1. It's written in essay form. It has an introduction, several paragraphs of proof, and a clear conclusion. However, it's also a creative piece that is not easily translatable into formulas or patterns.
2. It has a *focus:* the "Orphan Sock Enigma."
3. It is specific: the problem, the research, the chart and figure make it real and vivid.
4. This is a production piece that few seniors could do. However, if you can write with comparable flair and humor, it is a reasonable option for a college essay. It presents a good picture of the writer, his interest in science, his imagination and humor, how extensively he thinks about life, and how well he can write.

Sample 6

As a member of the Wesleyan community, I can contribute extensively both in and out of the classroom. As a student I am motivated to explore as many perspectives of as many different disciplines as I possibly can. I am fascinated by the creative potential of the human mind as well as by the complexities of the universe. I enjoy the challenge of expanding my store of knowledge and experiences, and the feeling of accomplishment when I have met the challenge successfully. This attitude enables me to be an active force in the classroom, continually questioning and discovering new parallels between diverse ideas.

My enthusiasm to discover extends beyond studying specific fields of knowledge to the experience of living. I like to be surrounded by people with a variety of backgrounds and interests. I am intrigued by their differences, and make an effort to be accepting of these differences. As a result, I feel that I may be able to pull together students with different points of view. Interpersonal relationships are very important to me. I believe that communication and responsibility are the two most important elements in all human relationships. I value honesty, integrity, and frankness as well as sensitivity and empathy for other people and I hope to receive the same respect in turn.

It is very important for me to devote some of my time to helping others. During college I intend to continue to take an active role in social action programs. In addition to serving the community at large, I feel a personal responsibility to take an equally active role in creating a better environment for myself and others. I plan to be involved in student government and other organizations that work to this end. I hope that my personal commitment enourages the commitment to attempt productive social change.

Things To Notice About This Essay

1. It does not use a standard essay form. Since there is no real body here, the first paragraph cannot be said to introduce, nor the last to conclude. In fact, all three paragraphs are pretty much interchangeable.
2. There is a *focus:* what the writer has to offer Wesleyan.
3. There is no *proof.* There are no specifics about either the writer or the school.
4. It is full of clichés, generalizations, and lofty language and it could apply to nearly any high school senior. It does not add to the application; it is truly forgettable.
5. It does not show a strong effort to go beyond the surface aspects of the topic. It is general and therefore reveals almost nothing about the writer.

Sample 7

I used to be a pretty deep guy. I watched foreign films, read Nietzsche, and stayed up all night "contemplating jazz." I was Jack Kerouac living in a fire hut on top of Desolation Peak. I was Gary Snyder seeking enlightenment in a Buddhist monastery in Thailand. I was Ken Kesey, Jimi Hendrix, and Timothy Leary all rolled up in one gigantic mess of pseudo-intellectual, adolescent, fancy boarding school beat poet wannabe. I was a moron.

I blew off my schoolwork not because I was lazy, but because I thought that schoolwork was shallow, too insignificant for me, the vivacious intellectual, the dharma bum, the Zen lunatic wanderer. How could my teachers expect me to do their homework, when life around me was all so futile, so meaningless? I was sure that I was a tortured soul destined to lead a life full of angst and pain.

That was last fall, more than a year ago now. In February of last year, I left my hipster friends and their coffee-house conversations behind, to move back to the suburbs of Philadelphia and my conservative, unhip public high school. Suburban Philadelphia is not the easiest place in the world to be sixties cool and stylish. There aren't many smoke-filled coffee houses or hippie wanderers. It's clean here, upper middle class—you know, the Ford Explorer, Saturday evening Mass, country club for dinner scene. I came back to Philadelphia because it isn't all that "hip," because there is nothing "profound" to do. I came home to get myself together. It was time to grow up.

I'm not as cool as I used to be. I never do anything very exciting or off the wall, at least not by my old standards. My friends from boarding school have for the most part become nothing more than distant memories. They're all off in New York

City or Mexico pretending to work on their spirituality, but really just partying their lives away. I stay home a lot. I'm at the library a couple of nights a week. I read, I write letters, I do some painting.

Last weekend, I watched *The Color Purple* with my mom, collected some weather data for a chemistry project, and had a tea party with my little sister. I've been spending time with the people I met in my high school production of *Arsenic and Old Lace*, too. I feel balanced; I feel like myself. I no longer want to tend bar in Tangiers or meditate in Sri Lanka . . . all right, maybe I do, but not right now. For so long, I wanted to be other people, to be a cultural icon, a legend in my own time. But in reality, I'm nothing like Keith Richards. Honestly, I'm a little scared of sex and drugs. I worry about pimples, whether my parents are still happily married, where I'm going to be next year.

I came home, I grew up, I got my life back together. I'm still trying to find a balance, but I no longer feel like a reckless child. I was sure that I could get away from myself by just pretending that I was someone else. But right now, I'm not looking to be "on the road." I'm pretty happy being right where I am.

Things To Notice About This Essay

1. The story this writer tells seems sincere. It explains things from his transcript: a change of schools, improving grades.
2. The essay expects the reader to know all the references here to people (Gary Snyder, Keith Richards) and literature (*On the Road*, Dharma Bums, the line from poet Alan Ginsberg about "contemplating jazz.") The writer has a real depth of knowledge, which is good, but in some of these references, he may be expecting a little too much from the reader . . . who won't be 17.

3. The essay has a clear focus ("It was time to grow up"), extensive use of specifics and descriptive details, and a strong sense of a writer who has thought about his life experiences.

4. The essay doesn't follow a traditional organization pattern and there are a few liberties with word choice and spelling ("wannabe"). A bit of a "risk," this essay does match a writer who himself has taken chances. He tells *his* story with grace and conviction.

Sample 8

As a seventeen year old, I don't yet have the experience or vision to know exactly what I want to accomplish beyond the turn of the century. What I hope college will do for me is to broaden my base of knowledge with a solid liberal arts education. I would like to have the power to explore Drake's equation for extraterrestrial life while at the same time analyzing the similes used in Virgil's *Aeneid*. Or maybe I could investigate the applications of integral calculus or the themes of self-sacrifice in Shakespeare. From the combination of courses I decide to take, I expect to find one or two true passions that I can extract from the rest and expand my knowledge exponentially in that field.

While I am working towards an academic concentration, I would like to focus my athletic efforts on swimming. At Springfield High, my intense training in swimming is interrupted every winter by my commitment to the basketball team. I am confident that concentrating solely on swimming will enable me to improve my past performances and times. If I could post a University record at Blodgett Pool and also find those one or two academic passions, I will have attained what I wanted from Princeton. And I am hopeful that in combining and completing these goals, I will have given something back to the school.

Things To Notice About This Essay

1. The writer's use of specific topics from a liberal arts curriculum suggests that she has thought about what's going to go on in college (Drake, Virgil, calculus, Shakespeare). Weaker sentences are those lacking specifics (Sentence 2: "broaden my base of knowledge with a solid liberal arts education." Final sentence: "combining and completing these goals, I will have given something back to the school").

2. The writer is honest about her plans and her ability to predict a future at least four years away. But she is also positive about what she's isn't sure of, emphasizing the future possibilities rather than her indecision.

3. It's a good idea to show a familiarity with the buildings and programs of the school to which you're applying. But if you write several essays like this one, be sure to proofread carefully. Isn't Blodgett pool at Harvard?

Sample 9

I knew I was going to Pittsburgh to play in a tournament. I didn't know I would be visiting Houston, Pennsylvania between matches. A rural suburb twenty miles outside the city's industrial hub, Houston is my father's hometown.

His family, he says, was "dirt poor" and barely able to sustain the house we found still standing—tired of living, it seemed, and shedding its blue paint. My father pointed to a street corner blanketed with scattered sections of a local paper: "It was there . . . right there . . . where I stood and looked around me and saw that my future was contained in this town. It was painful to think of leaving. That street corner was the center of my universe." My father was the first person in his family—the first person in the little mining town—to go to college.

As my father drove me along the unpaved back roads, he tried to find messages and axioms in the half-century old tale, but they did not answer the chain of questions jerked along by my consciousness: *How did he get out? Why did he come back? Why did he want to bring me here? Can I be as proud of my life as he is of his? What do I have to accomplish to gain such satisfaction? Do I have to do it soon?*

His stories stacked on top of each other likes books on a desk. Each anecdote was another volume from his childhood and I was struggling to keep up with the reading. We passed the old house six times before he was ready to separate himself from Houston this time. The children playing outside the house tried to examine us through the tinted glass of our rented Luxury Town Car and I shifted uncomfortably in my bucket seat. *What opportunities did they have? What would I do with mine?*

"Dad, these people are going to call the police if we keep circling the block."

Back at our hotel in Pittsburgh, I shouldered my racquet bag and followed my father up the staircase to our room. On each step, I tried to plant my foot exactly where he had put his.

Things To Notice About This Essay

1. The organization is basically narrative. The writer's insights and reflections are incorporated into the story of her visit to Houston.
2. The writer does not tell the reader what this experience means. It's a risk, but she assumes we will figure out the connection between her father's experiences and her own. The italicized section in the middle guides the reader in understanding the end.

3. The writer supplies the details needed to create a picture of the place. The use of realistic dialogue adds credibility.
4. The essay tells only a small story but it reveals the writer's ability both to think about her own experiences and to understand the experiences of other, different people.

Sample 10

Pocahontas is playing every hour on the hour this week. The theater teems with ornery, hyperactive kids for the half hour before each show. We have thirty minutes between each surge to sweep the floors of the concession stand before the next wave arrives to plead with their parents for four-dollar plastic buckets of junk food.

For $4.75 an hour after taxes (a little more than one of those buckets costs), it isn't the best summer job and it only feels like the worst when *Pocahontas* is playing. Usually we have plenty of time between shows to sweep up popcorn and replenish cups, buckets, and lids from the strangely-shaped cupboards underneath the counter where you have to grope blindly while on your knees. It's even more exciting when looking for the vats of simulated butter, which leave ominous oil-and-artificial-flavoring cakes on the bottom of the shelves. I used to order "butter topping" with my movie popcorn. After one day of pouring vats of it into the heating and dispensing machine, I decided I could never order it again.

I wish I could say it has been an educational experience, that it has made me a better person, or that for whatever reason I am secretly Forrest Gump. But the truth is that I spent the summer in an airconditioned theater with free movies to earn enough money to pay for gas. And during the summer, that's all that matters in a teenager's world.

Things To Notice About This Essay

1. Asked to write about his summer activities, this writer tells the truth about his job in a clever and entertaining way.
2. There is no great lesson being taught but still the essay offers a clear focus—what he did last summer—and specifics that make that experience vivid and memorable to the reader.
3. The writer uses irony in the contrast of his wages and the pop-corn purchases. He uses humor in explaining his recent decision to swear off "butter topping." Small touches like this are just enough (he's not applying to clown college).
4. Although the writer says he hasn't learned anything at the movies, his essay suggests he has thought carefully about his experience and can write about it clearly and with wit.

Sample 11

A person who influenced me me was Mrs. Baldwin, my best friend's mother. Mrs. Baldwin was always around whenever I went over to see Stacey. She was form Alabama and she always looked up from whatever she was making and said "Hey girl" to me when I came in the kitchen door. I was shocked when my Mom told me that Mrs. Baldwin had cancer. I couldn't believe that anyone I knew, anyone I cared about, could be dying.

It was very hard for everyone as Mrs. Baldwin got sicker. I think her whole family was in shock. She went to the hospital for treatments and for chemotherapy but I knew that things weren't getting better.

Mrs. Baldwin died at home just before Thanksgiving last year. I still think about her often and I know things are completely different for her kids and for her husband. Stacey and I don't ever talk about it but I can tell things have changed.

When Mrs. Baldwin died, I realized that people aren't forever. I know now that we all have to appreciate each other while we can. I think I've changed and I believe that Mrs. Baldwin has had a significant impact on my life. She gave me so much. She gave me a chance to laugh, to tell my stories, and to feel welcomed. She gave me the ability to be myself. Wherever I go, I know that Mrs. Baldwin will be watching over me, helping me to be happy.

Things To Notice About This Essay

1. It is very hard to write about death. Poets and playwrights have been struggling—and often failing—for centuries. Think long and hard before you assign yourself the task of writing in a meaningful and fresh way about illness or death.
2. The essay has a clear focus: Mrs. Baldwin was important to the writer. A bit of specific evidence is offered: the friendly "Hey girl." The reader wonders what other things Mrs. Baldwin did, what conversations they had, what actions created the feelings of warmth and closeness.
3. The writer uses a chronological organization and tells the story toward a conclusion ("I realized . . ."). The essay is organized, but the conclusion isn't completely persuasive. Compare Sample 3 or 9, both of which tell more specific stories to support their conclusions. Remember to show rather than tell.
4. A final version of this essay should include revisions of "completely different," "so much," and "be myself." The reader needs help to visualize what these phrases mean.
5. The writer may have used a spell-checking program but errors like those in lines one and three show she didn't proofread.

I do not recommend any of these essays to you as models. I present the eleven as examples of the strengths (focus, proof, simple language, structure, vividness) and weaknesses that have been discussed throughout this book. It is irrelevant what schools these essays were written for or whether the applicants were accepted. But as an important part of the overall performance and impression of an application, your essay matters. A look at these samples may help you avoid the pitfalls, enjoy the variety, and end up with an essay that gives a connected, strong, and vivid picture of you to the colleges of your choice.

Suggested Reading

Barnet, Sylvan. *A Short Guide to Writing About Literature.* 7th ed. New York: HarperCollins Publishers, 1996.

Corbett, Edward P. J. and Sheryl L. Finkle. *The Little English Handbook: Choices and Conventions.* 6th ed. New York: HarperCollins, 1992.

Gibaldi, Joseph, and Walter S. Achtert. *MLA Handbook for Writers of Research Papers.* 4th ed. New York: Modern Language Association, 1995.

Hacker, Diana. *A Writer's Reference.* 3rd ed. Boston: Bedford Books, 1995.

Strunk, William, Jr., and E. B. White. *The Elements of Style.* 3rd ed. Boston: Allyn and Bacon Publishers, 1995.

Trimble, John. *Writing with Style: Conversations on the Art of Writing.* Englewood Cliffs, N.J.: Prentice Hall, Inc., 1974.

Zinsser, William. *On Writing Well: An Informal Guide to Writing Nonfiction.* 5th ed. New York: HarperCollins Publishers, 1995.

Preparation for College: From the College Board

College Board. *The College Board Guide to 150 Popular Majors.* New York: College Entrance Examination Board, 1992.

College Board. *College Costs and Financial Aid Handbook* (current edition of annual publication). New York: College Entrance Examination Board.

College Board. *The College Handbook* (current edition of annual publication). New York: College Entrance Examination Board.

College Board. *Index of Majors and Graduate Degrees* (current edition of annual publication). New York: College Entrance Examination Board.

College Board. *10 Real SATs.* New York: College Entrance Examination Board, 1997.

Gelband, Scott, Catherine Kubale, and Eric Schorr. *Your College Application,* Updated and Revised. New York: College Entrance Examination Board, 1991.

Hartman, Kenneth E. *Internet Guide for College-Bound Students.* New York: College Entrance Examination Board, 1996.

Mitchell, Joyce Slayton. *The College Board Guide to Jobs and Career Planning.* New York: College Entrance Examination Board, 1994.

Note: To order College Board books via the Internet, visit College Board Online at www.collegeboard.com.

Index